"There are few people I have met who can ignite the ~~imag~~ ... ~~e~~ does. Inside her diminutive frame is the power of the universe, proof of the divine. I believe she is an instrument of God's love and guidance."
—Kelsey Grammer, producer of *Medium*

"In the more than twenty-five years I've known Yolana, it's not just her accuracy, but also her outstanding attitude about life that I have found so uncanny."
—William Norwich, columnist for *Vogue*

"Without a doubt, ninety percent accurate in all she says . . . an amazing gift. Working together was truly mind-boggling."
—Captain Richard Riguzzi, Harrison, New York,
Police Department (retired)

"I love Yolana. She has given me a fantastic opportunity to broaden my horizons and enrich my life."
—Detective Sergeant Dennis E. Bootle,
New York City Police Department

"Yolana has diagnosed in people what other doctors overlooked. In one case, she sent a man to me who did not speak English and she said he was about to have a stroke. This was after his doctor's exam, and the man's doctor said he was fine. Upon entering my office, he was found to have an abnormal heart rhythm that is known to cause strokes. I believe she saved this man's life. Amazingly gifted."
—Evan S. Levine, M.D., cardiologist
and author of *What Your Doctor Won't (or Can't) Tell You*

"As an artist, I am always looking for the spiritual in life, wanting to deepen my perceptions and sense of truth. When you meet Yolana, her warmth and extreme sensibility embrace your soul, and a sense of well-being surrounds you. Honesty and love are what you leave with."
—Robert Davi, actor

"Yolana seems very down-to-earth about her psychic abilities, and her enjoyable book reads a bit like a charming aunt telling you the story of her life."
—*Library Journal*

Just One More Question

ANSWERS AND INSIGHTS
FROM A PSYCHIC MEDIUM

Yolana

with

Mark Bego

Foreword by Hans Holzer

Berkley Books, New York

THE BERKLEY PUBLISHING GROUP
Published by the Penguin Group
Penguin Group (USA) Inc.
375 Hudson Street, New York, New York 10014, USA
Penguin Group (Canada), 90 Eglinton Avenue East, Suite 700, Toronto, Ontario M4P 2Y3, Canada (a division of Pearson Penguin Canada Inc.)
Penguin Books Ltd., 80 Strand, London WC2R 0RL, England
Penguin Group Ireland, 25 St. Stephen's Green, Dublin 2, Ireland (a division of Penguin Books Ltd.)
Penguin Group (Australia), 250 Camberwell Road, Camberwell, Victoria 3124, Australia (a division of Pearson Australia Group Pty. Ltd.)
Penguin Books India Pvt. Ltd., 11 Community Centre, Panchsheel Park, New Delhi–110 017, India
Penguin Group (NZ), Cnr. Airborne and Rosedale Roads, Albany, Auckland 1310, New Zealand (a division of Pearson New Zealand Ltd.)
Penguin Books (South Africa) (Pty.) Ltd., 24 Sturdee Avenue, Rosebank, Johannesburg 2196, South Africa

Penguin Books Ltd., Registered Offices: 80 Strand, London WC2R 0RL, England

PRINTING HISTORY
Putnam hardcover edition / March 2006
Berkley trade paperback edition / February 2007

Berkley trade paperback ISBN: 978-0-425-21372-8

The Library of Congress has catalogued the Putnam hardcover edition as follows:

Yolana, 1940–.
Just one more question: answers and insights from a psychic medium / Yolana with Mark Bego.
p.   cm.
ISBN 0-399-15309-8
1. Yolana, 1940–.   2. Psychics—United States—Biography.   I. Bego, Mark.   II. Title.
BF1027.Y65A3 2006   2005054953
133.8092—dc22
[B]

PRINTED IN THE UNITED STATES OF AMERICA

10 9 8 7 6 5 4 3 2 1

I dedicate this book to my children, who have gone through most of the good and bad times in my life and always made me smile.

I am proud of all my kids—they came from a hard stone. They have been through hell in the past, and they are all doing well today. My older son, Michael, is a doctor in Scarsdale. He is also gifted as a "healer," one of those people who can make other people well just by touching them. My younger son, Ronnie, is a psychic like me. He travels all over the world, giving advice and doing readings for people. He is one of the best in the world, and is also a highly respected businessman.

Then there's my daughter, Melody, who is a great mother. I have always felt that she has underestimated herself. She would have been a great lawyer, or a great actress. Like Ronnie, she is very psychic. However, she doesn't want anything to do with it, wouldn't go near it with a ten-foot pole. And I don't blame her. Not everyone has the patience or ability to answer that one more question.

As for my grandchildren, I've left these lessons to learn from.

Michael, Audrey, Ronald, Cheri, Melody, John, Daneé, Max-A-Million, Alexander, Noelani, Rebecca, and Sarah—this is for you.

Acknowledgments

I would like to acknowledge all the people who have come in and out of my life, and for all the lessons they have taught me. I would need many books to properly list them all. Here are just some of the people who are near and dear to me:

Josephine Sonnenblick, Elinor Esposito, Ben Auteri, Susan Summers, Diane von Furstenberg, Detective Jack Kennedy, Detective Richard Riguzzi, Dr. William Levin, Detective Dennis Bootle, Margaret Brewer, Ray and Philippa Hill, William Norwich, Andy Cordone, Kevin Lencki, Robert Davi, Kelsey and Camille Grammer, Rob Picarello, Denise Silvestro, Marilyn Ducksworth, Doc Levine, Psychic Media International, Sir Huw Shakeshaft, Leslie Gelbman, Chief Bowles, "Goumba Johnny" Sialiano, Steve and Jackie Baker, Detective Joe Comacho, Hans Holzer, Scott Barnes, Mark Kadillak, and my hairdresser, Ronnie, of Helio DeSouza.

In loving memory of Mitch Ducksworth.

Contents

Foreword

Yolana is probably the best medium in the world. I know many mediums, and I've tested many of them, so I have a right to say Yolana is the best. And, besides, it was I who found her in the first place, and persuaded her to pursue a career as a professional medium.

It all started some twenty or more years ago. At the time, Yolana was working for friends of mine, Mr. and Mrs. Gagen, as a domestic helper. Christina Gagen called me one day. "You know, this woman who works for me here at the house is extremely psychic," she said, "and I know you're interested in finding new mediums. She predicted a number of things that have actually come true. I think you ought to look into it."

Well, I did look into it, and I found what I consider the best deep trance medium in the world today. I spoke with Yolana at length, explaining the dos and don'ts of mediumship, and then suggested that she should make it her life's work.

Today, Yolana works both as a trance medium and as a clair-voyant. In other words, she has several "phases," as we say in the business, and she's good at all of them. Mediumship is a gift, of course, and she has learned to use it wisely and well.

Sometime after our initial encounter, I heard that Yolana had left the Gagens' employ and moved into the Martha Washington Hotel, where she not only was living but also giving readings by appointment. I kept up with her career because people kept telling me about the quality of her work, which was first-rate.

I would call on Yolana from time to time to work with me on particularly puzzling police cases, such as the time a police chief needed help solving a murder. He had some potential suspects lined up but no hard evidence.

I put Yolana into a deep trance during which the murder victim, believe it or not, spoke. The police lieutenant present told me that only the victim could have known some of the details of the case, details they needed to convict the person who committed the crime. From that day on, Yolana always has made herself available whenever the police need the help of a medium.

It has been many years since Yolana has been at the Martha Washington Hotel. Today, she lives in a very comfortable apartment on New York's Upper East Side. People still consult her for readings on a regular basis, including many A-list celebrities whose names I won't mention here.

This book is the first attempt to tell Yolana's life story since she has become the number one medium in the world. There are other talented psychics, yes, and there are even psychics who don't know they have the gift, but none of them measures up to Yolana. She reveals information to her clients that has substantive meaning for them, something that any psychic can do, but Yolana is very accurate. And while she's not one hundred percent accurate in her readings—no psychic is—she is the most gifted of any medium I've ever worked with.

I have worked with Yolana on many cases, and I can attest to her talent. This book will acquaint the world with her gift and with her accomplishments. I hope she will be with us for many years to come, to not only help those who have lost loved ones and need psychic advice but also to serve as a fount of information.

One word of advice to people wishing to consult Yolana: she is very busy, and you may not be able to get an appointment right way. Be patient. When you get the appointment, you will not be disappointed.

And a word of caution: don't volunteer names or information that could be construed as helping the psychic contact the person you have lost or give you the information you are seeking. Your job as the client is to ask for the reading, nothing more. You should just sit with the medium and wait to see what he or she will tell you. Sometimes you will receive the information you are hoping for, sometimes not. But volunteering information will make the reading invalid.

When you meet Yolana and get a reading, you will know why I call her the best. I'm glad to have been instrumental in discovering her, or perhaps it was she who found me. Either way, we have been together for many years, and we still work together occasionally and are still friends. And her son Ronald also has the gift, but that's another book.

Having a psychic gift is not a supernatural phenomenon. Intuition is a natural and normal human trait that all people have—some more, some less—Yolana has much, much more.

—*Dr. Hans Holzer*
Parapsychologist and author

Just

One More

Question

Introduction

My name is Yolana, and I am a professional psychic. Some people might call what I do "fortune-telling" or "soothsaying" or "spiritual advising," but I feel I simply read the visions that I see, listen to the voices that I hear, and interpret the messages that I receive when I tap into the spirit world. Spirits are all around us, but not everyone can feel their presence, let alone see or hear them. I do.

Sometimes, I can see what is going to happen long before it actually happens. Other times, I see things which have already occurred——things that other people desperately wish to know, such as who committed a particular crime or where a missing child is. This gift of being able to communicate with the spirit world is not something that I learned or was taught. It has always been a part of me.

Although I was surrounded by psychic phenomenon as a child, I never foresaw a career for myself as a psychic. I was interested in other things, like becoming a Rockette at Radio City Music Hall, for instance. But that dream wasn't going to materalize, not with the life I led as a child. I came from a broken home. My father was always running around with other women and my mother was an alcoholic. Neither one of them had the time or inclination to manage the career of an aspiring "star." Hell, some days they had trouble managing themselves.

So instead of becoming a child star on Broadway, I wound up having a child of my own at the age of fourteen. Early motherhood led to all kinds of problems, especially with my boyfriend's parents, who enjoyed tormenting me even after he and I got married. After we divorced years later, my luck didn't get any better. I wound up with a man who was clinically depressed and who one day tried to strangle me with his bare hands. I hit rock bottom then, and at the age of thirty-seven I found myself broke, turned away by everyone I knew, and living on the streets of New York City. I begged for money and slept in the subway. I had lost everything, including my three children.

But through it all, I knew God put me on this earth for a reason. I never lost my will to live, to go on. Even when I was on the absolute bottom rung of life's ladder, I knew that the only way to go was up. And from that lowest point, I began to put my life back together. That was when I really began to develop my psychic powers in earnest. I moved into a welfare hotel, and, to make ends meet, gave psychic readings in the coffee shop downstairs.

When word got out that I could communicate with the spirit world and give people a glimpse of what the future had in store for them, it wasn't long before a virtual who's who of the rich and famous began to seek me out. Bit by bit, I put my life back together. Today, I am told, I am ranked as one of the top psychic advisors in the world.

Communicating with the spirit world isn't always a bed of roses, but it's what I was put on this earth to do. Spirits know who can hear them, and they know how to find us. Sometimes I get visited by a disgruntled spirit in the middle of the night, and I have to tell them point-blank, "Get the hell out of here. I have my own problems to deal with."

My life has been a roller coaster of extreme highs and lows, but I have never lost my perspective on who I am and where I am going. It is this perspective that I try to convey to my clients who are seeking direction.

People come to me with questions about their lives, what the future has in store for them. And I give them answers. But after every reading, without fail, they ask me, "Can I ask you just one more question?" No matter what I've told them, they always have that one last question. And even after I answer that one, invariably they have just one more.

I try to answer all the questions my clients ask, but I also try to make them see that no one has all the answers. I believe we are all put on this earth to learn, so I try to help them see that they should be more concerned about learning who they are and why God put them here instead of worrying about getting their lover back or whether or not they should sell their house. Discovering who you are and what your purpose is is more important than anything else. It's also important to understand what you've been through because that prepares you for what is to come. Understanding why you repeatedly go through the seemingly same crisis keeps you from having to go through it yet again.

Although I am able to help people get answers to questions about their lives, I don't think of myself as better or more powerful than anybody else. I feel that we all have psychic powers, but ninety-nine percent of the population either does not pay attention to the signs and the voices around them or is not comfortable enough to follow their own instincts. Not everyone is cut out to be a psychic. I often say God gave all of us the ability to dance, but we all can't be ballerinas.

To help people get in touch with their psychic abilities, I teach classes in psychic awareness. Once students are aware of their abilities, I can help them sharpen their skills. From day one, I stress that the mind has to be opened, not closed. I can't conduct classes with skeptics—I end up answering their questions and arguing with them the whole time. Don't get me wrong: I'm not afraid of the skeptics or their questions; as a matter of fact, I welcome both. But there's a place for such people and their questions and the classroom is not it. When I teach, everyone has to be opened to the same page; otherwise, the class wouldn't work. I can't teach in an atmosphere of closed negativity.

I want my students to use their own brains. I tell them all the time that while I may know more about things psychic than they do, I don't know everything. Nobody knows everything there is to know. We are all learning all the time. I challenge my students to tap into their own abilities, and, over time, they find that they are able to answer their own questions. They become comfortable enough with their own gifts that they don't have to rely on mine. And in tapping into their own abilities, my students have even taught me a thing or two over the years.

Although my life story and parts of this book involve dark, even tragic matters, I feel that I had to experience or be exposed to them in order to become the person I am today. Through it all, I have never lost my sense of humor. My ability to laugh has helped me get through the tough times. It has also helped me deal with the nonbelievers I come across, who, I admit, I love to prove wrong every chance I get.

One particular instance that comes to mind is when I was consulted by police about the discovery of a male corpse with no head, no arms, and no legs, just a torso. When I was brought to the morgue to view the remains, the officers lifted up the sheet covering the corpse, expecting me either to be shocked or dumbfounded, but, to their surprise, I was neither. I simply turned to one of them, pointed to the well-endowed penis, and said: "Damn shame. This is a *big* loss for somebody!" I then went on to fill them in on all the details behind the unsolved murder. They were speechless.

After all that I have been through, I can honestly say that I am a survivor. I continue to communicate with the afterlife, and I work with a huge clientele that includes not only movie stars, politicians, and the wealthy but regular people who are trying to find their own way through life's maze. I have gone from the top to the bottom and back again. And most of my experiences have been not only unconventional but thoroughly entertaining as well. On the pages that follow, I want to share my story with you and what I've learned along the way.

ONE

Family

Business

I was born into a family of Hungarian Gypsies on April 11, 1940, in Yonkers, New York, and named Diane Elaine Lassaw. As a child, I was surrounded by the paranormal—in fact, my whole childhood seemed to revolve around spirits and fortune-telling. My mother was very in tune psychically, and she always seemed to be telling someone's fortune. But she didn't use an ordinary set of Tarot cards or a standard playing deck when she did her readings; I remember her using an old deck of Hungarian cards. People were amazed by her abilities. I also had a pair of "aunts," Lala Nanie and Juju Nanie, who practiced witchcraft. They weren't blood relatives, but they were fascinating to be around. While normal families would gather around the table after dinner on the holidays for a hand of pinochle or rummy, mine would break out a deck of cards and give each other readings.

I didn't question it at the time because I thought it was what everybody did. Reading the future with a deck of cards or making the hands of a clock move or a doorknob turn just by thinking about it seemed ordinary to me. I thought everybody could do it, that there was nothing rare or supernatural, let alone abnormal, about it. Whatever you grow up with, you accept as normal. Little did I know that it was anything but normal!

I should have known that being a psychic medium was going to be my calling in life since I was exposed to this strange world at such an early age, but I was too busy dreaming about becoming a singer or dancer to even think about life in the hereafter beyond the stars. The only stars I was interested in were on stage and up on the silver screen. Betty Hutton, Doris Day, all those people I would see on the covers of the film magazines—that was what was important to me. Never in my wildest dreams did I imagine that, one day, I would be doing readings for celebrities like those.

I was born, like my family members, with the gift of being able to tell people about their past, present, and future. It's part of me. It's there all the time. It's another sense just like taste, smell, and touch. But sometimes it becomes torture. Sometimes things enter my head and I can't shut them out, no matter how hard I try. If a spirit wants to get a message through to me, he or she will, even if I don't want to see or hear the vision or message they have for me.

That's one reason I don't like traveling. Taking a bus, train, plane, or ship can be a very difficult, even painful, experience for me because I can pick up on what people around me are thinking. I know what's going on in their minds, what their intentions might be. For instance, on the subway in New York I could pick up on some thug looking to steal someone's purse. And that's a great burden to me, because, at sixty-five years of age, what am I going to do? Tackle the guy? I'm all for helping people in any way I can, but sometimes I can't help. At times like those this gift is a curse. That's why I don't like to go out that much.

I'll never forget a horrible experience I had in the 1980s on a plane to Germany. I had gotten a call from Hans Holzer, my psychic mentor, inviting me to lecture and give readings at an institute in Düsseldorf. Not only was I going to be paid for the work, I also was going to be housed in the home of some rich woman who was connected with the institute. I had said yes immediately, not just for the work but also because my son Ronnie was stationed at an army base in Germany at the time and I hadn't seen him in almost three years. Ronnie wrote every chance he got, but we hadn't seen each other face-to-face since he enlisted. He always had a way of making me laugh, and I missed having him around. I wanted to see him so much that I was willing to confront my fears and fly over the ocean for hours to do it.

As soon as the plane was over Germany, however, my worst nightmare came true. First, I started hearing faint noises, like people screaming in the distance. After looking around and seeing that no one was making noise anywhere near me, I got out of my seat and looked around the rest of the plane. Again, I came up empty-handed. Then I looked out the window, because I thought I heard something coming from out there, but I saw nothing but darkness since it was the middle of the night. I did my best to ignore the sounds, but the farther we got into Germany the louder they became. Now I was hearing not only screaming but automatic gunfire as well, like a machine gun. I started to panic, looking around frantically to see if any of the other passengers heard what I heard, but they seemed unfazed, reading or sleeping in their seats.

When next I looked out the window, I saw World War II bombers flying alongside our plane, and I thought I might be going insane. The rat-a-tat from the machine gun was now pounding my brain, and the sound of people screaming was coming closer and closer. Now the gunfire sounded like it was coming from right outside my window, and when I looked out, I saw flashes of light and explosions as clear as day. Not wanting to lose control, I closed my eyes, hoping it would all go away, but it wouldn't. I started moaning softly and twisting in my seat. The man seated next to me became concerned and asked, "Do you feel sick, ma'am? Do you need me to call someone?"

While I appreciated his concern, I couldn't answer. If I tried to explain what was happening, he'd think I was nuts. But even if he didn't, who was he going to call? There was nothing anyone could do. I was on my own, and I hated it.

You see, what I was experiencing was coming from some forty years earlier, when Adolf Hitler was in power in Germany. I was receiving a firsthand account of the horror: the guns, the bombs, and the wails of those tortured and put to death in the concentration camps. I sat with my eyes closed tight in sheer terror, praying for it all to just go away. But it wouldn't. It just kept coming and coming. I started seeing victims being told to remove their clothes and then herded to the showers. These frightened souls were being reassured by their captors that they were going to be okay, but I knew differently. I knew these people were being led to their death. "Stop! Stop!" I started screaming. But it didn't matter what I did, they were going to be killed anyway.

Hearing my screams, the man seated next to me once again inquired, "Ma'am, are you sure you're okay? Are you sick?"

At this point, I opened my eyes and whispered, "I'm fine. I'm just psychic."

I'm not sure if my answer eased his worries, but he excused himself, got up, and never returned. I freaked him out so much that he moved to another seat.

Experiences like these, while not always quite so extreme, are part of my everyday life as a psychic medium. So when people say they wish they had my gift, I say be careful what you wish for. Some days it seems more of a curse than a gift.

The incident on the airplane was only the beginning. I was just starting to learn how to use and strengthen my powers, and, with the help of Holzer, I was exposed to new experiences every day. Hell, everything was new for me. It hadn't been that long ago that I was living on the streets without a dime to my name. I didn't think I'd ever see my children again, and now here I was flying to Germany on someone else's dime, going to see my son.

I have to admit it wasn't easy going to Germany alone. If there was a way I could have seen Ronnie without having to get on a plane, I would have. I was also worried about what would happen once I got there. How was I going to get by without speaking a word of German?

No one from the institute met me at the airport when I landed, so there I was all on my own. I was all dressed up with someplace to go but no way to get there. Hans had provided me with an address and written directions to the house where I was staying, but how was I going to find it? Sure, I could hail a cab, and show the driver the address, but what if he couldn't read English? Yet when I finally got a cab, I found I could speak enough German to make myself understood, even though I had never uttered a word of German before in my life! Even more amazing, not only could I give directions, I was able to carry on a conversation with the driver and understand every word he said. Amazing!

We arrived at the house in Düsseldorf, and while it looked charming from the outside, soon enough I learned that this house was anything but charming—it was haunted. So now I was going to have a ghost for a roommate. That freaked me out because I was not yet fully developed as a trance medium, that is, a psychic who can "channel" spirits. I had never communicated with those who had "passed over." Holzer would later help me more fully explore this gift, but at the time I was frightened by the ghostly activity that was going on in that little house. But I kept it to myself, and went about doing what I was hired to do.

While the institute provided me with an interpreter for readings, once I got there I decided I really didn't need one. German names, places, and phrases kept rolling off my tongue, a surprise to me, and to everyone around me since Hans had told my hosts that I didn't speak a word of their language.

A reading I did for a man really made the trip worthwhile. His wife had been ill for some time, and he had taken her to all the top specialists in Germany, but no one could pinpoint what was wrong. The concerned man told me his wife was losing more strength, and more hair, with each passing day. He worried she was running out of hope, and out of time.

Hearing his story, I immediately sensed the presence of a rock near his wife's chair. Even though it seemed an odd thing to see, I questioned him about it anyway. You see, even if what I see, or hear, seems strange to me I never discount it. The rock and chair provided a very important clue concerning the woman's health. The man told me he had found a beautiful rock a while back— one of the most interesting objects he'd ever seen—and given it to his wife as a gift. She loved it so much that she placed it on a table next to her chair so she could admire it all the time. She spent a lot of time in that chair, he went on to explain, because she worked from home. She was constantly in the presence of the rock.

I told him to have the rock tested. He looked at me like I was off my rocker but did it anyway. It turned out that the rock was radioactive, and that it was the radioactivity that was making his wife ill. Then the man had the whole house tested. Even the coffee his wife was drinking every day in that room was contaminated; setting the coffee cup next to the rock was all it took.

While I was more than happy to help this couple, a few nights later I was looking for someone to help me. I awoke in the middle of the night in that "charming" little house with white smoke coming out of my mouth! It terrified me, and I couldn't move my body for what seemed like hours. I had no idea what was happening to me or what to do about it. All I knew was, there was some kind of energy in the room because the windows began to rattle. In an effort to stop the rattling, and the smoke from coming out of me, I started to concentrate on my own energy, trying to pull the smoke back into my mouth. After a while, things calmed down. The rattling stopped, the smoke disappeared, and I was able to move my body once again. I frantically telephoned Hans to tell him what had happened. I told him it was one of the most frightening experiences of my life and that I was afraid to go back to sleep. He told me not to worry, that the white smoke was "ectoplasm," a substance released from a medium's body when a spirit wishes to make its presence known.

Great. Not only was I rooming with a ghost, this friggin' spirit matter could come out of my mouth whenever it wanted to communicate.

While Holzer's explanation calmed me down somewhat, I still wasn't totally at ease. Knowing for sure there was a spirit in the room with me didn't make me any more comfortable. In fact, just the opposite. Plus, there were other things going on in that house. Every time I tried to fall asleep, I felt someone or something stroking my hair. With Holzer in America, I was on my own. So I tried sleeping with the lights on. The people at the institute must have been thinking, *Some psychic medium this one is. She's afraid of the dark.* But I didn't care. I was creeped out.

By far, the best part of the trip was seeing Ronnie. He came to visit me at the house in Düsseldorf. When I laid eyes on him for the first time, I didn't recognize him: he was as thin as a rail, and wearing the most hideous clothes I had ever seen. You would have thought our first greeting in almost three years would have been something sentimental or even profound, but, no, my first words were: "What the hell are you wearing?" I asked him if he was working for the Salvation Army instead of the U.S. Army and if he had a mirror back at the base. Then we both had a good laugh.

Ronnie stayed at the house for a few nights. I told him what had been going on: not only the stroking of my hair but the feeling that someone was sitting on the bed with me, the rushes of cold air even though the windows were shut tight, and especially the visions of the scared Allied soldiers hiding out in the attic during the war. It was all so terrible and unbelievable that I had to share it with someone I knew before it made me crazy. But I think it was too much for Ronnie to handle at the time. He didn't really know how much I had developed my psychic ability since last we'd seen one another, and he certainly didn't know that I was making my living as a psychic. He had never been exposed to anything like he was witnessing in that haunted house, and, after a few nights, it got to him and he returned to the base as fast as he could.

On the other hand, as I began to understand what was happening it became less frightening to me. As I became more in tune with my psychic powers and the supernatural world, I felt more comfortable with what I was experiencing. It didn't make me any less afraid of the dark, however. To this day, if I feel there's a ghost in the room, I still insist on sleeping—if I can sleep at all—with the lights on.

We have all had the sensation at one time or another that something is present with us but we don't know what it is. While it's probably something you can't figure out on your own, rest assured that it *is* something. You're not paranoid or crazy. You just haven't developed your own psychic powers enough to recognize what it is. Now, I don't want you to get freaked out every time you get the willies. It could simply be one of your relatives who has crossed over dropping by to say hello. Whoever it is, no need to worry. Ghosts can be mischievous, wacky, even a nuisance, but they can't hurt you.

Over the years, I've learned to put these different phenomena in perspective. I try not to mind the noises, the movements. But, in all honesty, you never really get used to ghosts, even if you deal with them on a daily basis like I do. But for me, it's just another day at the office, only this office is haunted.

TWO

Facing
Your
Demons

*I*n life, we all have to face our demons at one time or another. Some of us are fortunate enough to recognize these demons early on and get them out of our lives as quick as they came, while others may not be so lucky. Exorcising demons from one's life is a tough task. Some people attack them head-on while others ignore them and therefore are never quite free of them.

The first step in pulling these thorns from our side is recognizing them. Look back to see when and where these demons became part of your life. Then you have a clue to determine *why* they became part of your life.

My troubles all started at an early age. Around the time that I was ten, my mother and my father's marriage began falling apart.

Their fighting escalated to the point of no return, my father left my mother, and they eventually divorced.

I really missed my father after he left, and always wanted to see him much more than I did. My mother, on the other hand, wanted nothing to do with him. In an attempt to heal her own wounds from my father's desertion, she began dating a series of men. She wanted to erase the memory of him, and she thought new men would help do that.

My mother was filled with such rage after my father left that she'd say such things as, "I hate you because you look like your father." She was right: I did look like my father, but that was no reason to hate me. It really shook me to the core when she said that. I don't know if she was purposely trying to hurt me, but she did. To this day, I often wonder how a mother could ever say such a thing to her own child. I understand his leaving caused her much pain, but I had nothing to do with it. It was *their* problem. But she took out her frustrations on me anyway. So while my mother turned to men, I turned to cigarettes, smoking an occasional cigarette or two.

A year after my father left, my mother met Tony Cacace, a nut job, who she ended up marrying. Almost every day, he would go to the store that my mother owned and take all of the money out of the cash register. He soon drained us dry financially. At eleven years of age, I dealt with all the bill collectors. They would call the store constantly and I would have to invent excuse after excuse about where my mother was and why the bills weren't being paid. It was a complete nightmare for me, but I had no choice because my alcoholic mother wasn't able to do it herself.

My life was so frustrating at that time that I soon came up with my own, quiet ways of rebelling against my mother. First it was cigarettes; I would constantly sneak out to smoke. A few years later, I turned to boys. My first real boyfriend, Bernie Bard, came into the picture when I was thirteen.

When I met Bernie, we seemed to have a lot in common. Our parents were shopkeepers, mine owning three different stores, Bernie's owning a jewelry store in Harlem. It wasn't at the stores that I met him, however, but on a blind date. Bernie was supposed to go out with my sister Paula and I was supposed to go out with some other guy, but somehow we ended up together. I was really too young to be dating back then, but I didn't care. I just wanted to get out of the house, and he was the ticket.

Bernie was a simple, uncomplicated guy. He was a good person and had a kind heart. Even though he was five years older than me, he was a bit childish for his age. But I didn't mind because I really liked him. However, it only led to bad things for me later.

As I started seeing Bernie more often, I began plotting how I was going to get out of my mother's house for good. I had had it with all of the nonsense—the booze and Tony's antics were really getting the best of me—and I couldn't stand living there much longer. Not a day went by without some horrific episode or another. I had finally gotten to the point where enough was enough.

Before I knew it, I was pregnant, at the age of fourteen, with my first son, Michael. But instead of giving me a way out of the house and a new life, it gave me all kinds of new problems and heartache instead. Remember, this was the 1950s, and in those days it was very different than it is today. Nowadays, you hear about pregnancy out of wedlock every day. Back then, it was rarely mentioned, let alone socially acceptable. Frequently, you were sent away to have the baby. You were a disgrace. I tried to hide my pregnancy for as long as I could, changing the tags on clothes I would buy so that no one would know what size I was wearing. I had always been heavy, so I could keep my secret for longer than most. It would come back to bite me when Michael was born, however.

I hid my pregnancy from everybody but Bernie right up to the very end, and I was in the hospital giving birth before anyone knew about it. I figured we'd work out such minor details as telling our parents and figuring out where we were going to live happily ever after once the baby was born. I knew that Bernie and I and the baby were going to be together; I just didn't know where.

When I finally did give birth to Michael, the beautiful experience of giving birth turned into a catastrophe. The Bards and my parents had never met one another before; there had been no reason to until then. So here they were, in the hospital room, seeing their grandson and meeting the family for the first time. It was quite a scene.

First, Bernie's parents came storming in. Then my mother made her grand entrance, strolling in like Lana Turner attending a movie premiere, wearing a big red picture hat that matched her red dress with its plunging neckline. To top it off, she was absolutely as drunk as a skunk. And my father showed up right behind her. God knows how she got hold of him!

The Bards acted as if they were in mourning, and my mother, dancing up and down the hallway, acted like it was a party, and, Lord knows, she never missed a party! It was a three-ring circus that only got worse once the baby was brought in by the nurse.

I was sharing a room with a black woman who gave birth at the same time as I did. When the smiling nurse walked into the room carrying a baby all wrapped in a blanket, she came over to me and handed the baby to me. Pulling the blanket back from the baby's face, I noticed no one else was smiling. As soon as I saw him, I knew why.

The baby I cradled in my arms was black, so I knew the nurse had made a mistake. Before I could say a word, however, the Bards almost had a collective heart attack right there. They were yelling all kinds of things at me, accusing me of lying to their son. But instead of explaining, I decided to give it right back. "He does look a little dark," I said. "I didn't know you had black genes in your family!" Well, that put them right over the edge. "That's *not* our son's child!" they screamed. "That's *not* our son's child!"

Obviously, the nurse gave me the wrong baby, giving the other mother my son instead. You should have heard the screaming going on on her side of the room! The nurse soon realized her mistake and switched babies. But that didn't resolve matters. Now the Bards realized their son had a child out of wedlock with a fourteen-year-old girl who wasn't Jewish! They started crying, carrying on like someone had just died, while my mother started to dance around again like she was the belle of the ball.

One reason the Bards were unhappy was their need to control. They were devout Jews who believed they were holier-than-thou and lived their lives by the book. Now, here was a situation over which they had no control. They looked ready to rip their clothes, as if they were in mourning. My mother's attitude, on the other hand, was, What can we do? The baby's here. Let's celebrate. And my father was also calm. He realized that there was nothing that he could do, so he just accepted the situation. Besides, he was remarried, and had started a new life of his own, so he'd already distanced himself somewhat from the whole scene.

The Bards just couldn't accept me—I was not the kind of girl they wanted their son to end up with. They wanted some devout, mousy Jewish girl who would sit at home and do as she was told. Guess what? That wasn't happening. They got me, and that was that.

After I got out of the hospital and with no place to go, Bernie and I wound up moving in with his parents. So I did get my wish and was finally out of my mother's house. But I immediately went from the frying pan into the fire. Living with the Bards was a disaster from the first day. They made it clear that they didn't want me there, and I couldn't deal with the rejection. So over the years Bernie and I bounced back and forth between the Bards' and my mother's house. Both options were a disaster, which did nothing for our baby, let alone our relationship.

Eventually, my father helped us get a one-bedroom apartment in Hilltop Acres, in Yonkers. Hard as we tried, it was really difficult to make ends meet. I was working at John Wanamaker's, in the candy department, while Bernie started up a watch repair business, and the Bards sat for Michael during the day.

When I was sixteen, Bernie and I decided to make it official and we got married. We couldn't marry in New York because I was still too young, so we ended up in Connecticut. We thought marrying would make everything perfect, but we soon realized that our union was anything but perfect. In fact, I started having an affair not long after, with a man known as "Turn 'Em Loose Bruce." To make matters worse, he was the Bards' lawyer.

There's never any good excuse to cheat on your spouse, but I was still a teenager who had a lot to learn about life, and I have to admit that Bruce taught me a lot. When we went out to dinner, he would tell me what to order off the menu. He would tell me how to behave when we went to a bar. He would tell me what was suitable and what was not, the kinds of things I never learned growing up. And he loved giving me advice. It was a lot like *My Fair Lady*: he was my Professor Higgins and I was his Eliza Doolittle. Plus, he had one of the most magnetic personalities of anyone I had ever met. I kept hoping he was going to divorce his wife and marry me, but that wasn't to be. In fact, I became pregnant with Bernie's second child, and that effectively put an end to any such wishes.

Ronnie was born on October 22, 1959, and we needed to get a bigger place than Hilltop Acres to accommodate us all. Once again, my father found an apartment at a place called the Cadillac Apartments, in Mount Vernon, New York. The boys each had his own bedroom, with Bernie and I sleeping on a tired old sofa in the living room. I really tried to do all I could to make a happy home, even getting a dog, a beagle. But even that proved disastrous; the dog wasn't all that bright, with the strange habit of getting its foot lodged in our Danish modern furniture.

Nothing was going right in my life. My relationship with my parents was strained; I couldn't stand my in-laws; I was the teenage mother of two children; I was cheating on my husband. As if that weren't enough, now I started seeing spirits and experiencing all sorts of other psychic phenomena. I seemed to be a magnet for it. Little did I know this was only the beginning. I was soon to exorcise some of the biggest demons in my life, and, in so doing, find my true calling.

While Bernie and I thought our move to the Cadillac Apartments would be great for our family, it wasn't. From the moment I walked through the door, I felt something just wasn't quite right, but I tried to ignore my feelings for the sake of my family. Little did I know my silence was putting them at risk. The Cadillac was possessed, and our place in particular was clearly in the grasp of some evil force.

Coming home late one night, I was to find out how on target my instincts were. Bernie, my brother Alan, and I pulled up to the building, and before we got out of the car I glanced up to our bedroom window to see if the lights were still on, wondering if the babysitter had put the kids to bed yet. My glance was met by the face of a stranger, not our babysitter. I pointed and screamed, and Bernie and Alan saw the face too. Fast-thinking Alan said, "Look, I'll go up the steps, you go up the elevator. If anyone is in there, we will catch whoever it is."

And that's what we did. With Alan heading up the steps, and Bernie and I heading up in the elevator, no one was going to get out of that building without running into one or the other of us. But when we got to our apartment, the babysitter was calmly sitting on the couch. Rushing into the bedroom, I found no one there. Back out in the living room, I asked the babysitter if anyone had been in the apartment with her. She shook her head no, and said that the kids had been asleep for a while and that she had been watching television by herself. There was no reason not to believe her; there was no indication that anyone had been here.

While I was glad everything was okay, I was still disturbed by what I had seen in the window. I knew what I saw. A girl, with dark circles under her eyes, dressed in what looked to be a sailor's uniform, the type of uniform schoolgirls used to wear at the turn of the century. That's what Bernie and Alan saw too. And while I never saw her again, or found out anything about her, I knew then that the Cadillac Apartments were truly haunted. Unfortunately, that was just the beginning of my experiences living there.

The scariest time was one night when I was alone in the bedroom. Happy to have some quiet time for myself, I decided to meditate and pray a little. I was in a very calm and contemplative mood, and I thought that meditating a bit and talking to God would do me some good. Boy, did I get the wrong number! The entity I connected with was anything but God.

I had lit a candle and placed it in front of the large mirror on the dresser. Then I gazed deeply into the mirror for some reason, and for as long as I live I'll never forget what I saw there.

I was leaning with my elbows on the dresser when suddenly the whole room went cold. The room began to fill with fog and a face popped up in the mirror out of nowhere. It was definitely *not* human. The head was square-shaped, with bloodred eyes, almost like those red eyes you see in flash photographs only a hundred time worse. What the hell is this!?! I thought to myself in sheer terror. My heart was racing a mile a minute, and I felt like I was going to be sick to my stomach. It was that vertigo kind of feeling you get when peering over the railing of a tall building. The face I saw was surely that of the devil himself.

Suddenly, this apparition let out a growl that shook me to the core and caused me to fall back onto the bed. Then it disappeared.

I lay there, shaken to the core. What had I summoned up from the depths of hell?

Whatever it was, it left its mark. The mirror remained fogged, unable to be cleared up no matter what I tried, even straight ammonia. The devil had burned the fog into that mirror.

As if seeing the devil weren't enough, another time I saw a man in our living room hanging from a noose. I was later to find out that there had been a suicide committed in that room. Apparently, the spirit of that dead man wanted me to know he was still around.

Living in the Cadillac Apartments quite literally brought me face-to-face with my inner demons. But I couldn't understand at the time what was happening. We had rented the place because we thought it would be better for us, but it seemed like it was forcing us out. It depressed me so much that I turned to another demon: alcohol. I drank alone, just like my mother, and, worse, I drank cheap Thunderbird wine. Now, *that's* evil!

Not being really in touch with my psychic powers, I had no idea how to handle the situation. Yes, I could see spirits, but I didn't know what my powers were. Instead, I dismissed what I saw and drowned my fears in the cheap wine.

We eventually moved back to Yonkers, to a one-bedroom apartment. Most comfortable of all, no more ghosts. But we had money issues. Bernie did his best to provide for us, but he just didn't make enough money repairing watches. So I began to resent Bernie.

I started having terrible nightmares about finding Bernie dead in bed. Every time I walked into the bedroom, I thought I would find my nightmare had come true. If I called the house when I went out and he didn't answer right away, I was sure he was dead. I would wake up in the middle of the night and check to make sure he was still breathing. The vision kept coming to me so regularly that I started to wonder if it could be a premonition.

Although I was afraid of Bernie dying, I came to realize that I was not in love with him. I was just a kid when we began dating. What did I know about life and love at the age of fourteen? I just wanted out of my mother's house. Now I was a young woman in my twenties with two kids and trapped in a life not of my own making.

It was then that I found myself falling in love with John Macdonald, a neighborhood doctor and a married man. I thought he was the answer to my prayers when I became pregnant with his child. He would leave his wife, I would leave Bernie, and we would marry. But things didn't work out as planned. John suddenly dropped dead two days after our Melody was born, leaving me now with three children and still married to Bernie. I knew life was full of lessons, but what was the lesson here? What was I supposed to be getting out of all this misery?

So many questions, but no one seemed to have any answers for me. One thing I did know was I wasn't about to tell Bernie that Melody wasn't his child. It would only make a bad situation worse.

After Melody was born, we moved again, this time to a house in Yonkers owned by Bernie's parents. They gave it to Bernie, with the expectation that he would pay all the bills while we lived there. That didn't last long. We got into debt again, and had to sell the house. After paying off the Bards' mortgage, Bernie and I split whatever was left over and went our separate ways.

Bernie was a terribly nice guy, but he was living in his own naive little world. If I would have told him that the moon was made of green cheese, he would have believed me. Unfortunately, that's not the kind of man I wanted to be married to.

A little after our breakup, Bernie met Ida, and they planned to get married once our divorce was final. But that never happened. Bernie died before our divorce was final. And just like in my premonition, he died in bed. The difference was, Ida was lying next to him instead of me.

After Bernie's death, my life went in a whole new direction, and at first I felt so alone. Even though Bernie and I were no longer together, he was always there for me to turn to. Now that he was gone, I realized what I had lost. I realized that we were both children when we met, and that we didn't know any better. But I also realized that he taught me a lot. He taught me what a good human being was. He taught me how to love, and how to be loved. He was a good soul.

At the funeral home, I made my peace with Bernie. I wasn't at all bitter. I was able to say good-bye with no regrets. In fact, I recalled all the good times we had together. I remembered going to Coney Island together, and him having my name tattooed on his bicep. I loved him then, and he loved me. Sure, we had many rough times, but we also had a lot of laughs together: the pillow fights, the dog running around with Bernie's underwear over his head—silly, fun times. All those memories came back to me at the funeral, and that made it all easier to cope with. Most of all, I knew in my heart that Bernie still loved me when he died. We just couldn't live together anymore.

I shocked everyone when I didn't cause a scene when Ida showed up. All eyes were glued on us, especially the Bards', as I walked right up to her and embraced her. He loved her, I told myself. Who am I to deny him that right?

Bernie lay there in his coffin, and I knew my buddy was gone forever. I knew there was nothing I could do to bring him back. The least I could do for him was to let go of any anger I might be harboring and be there for his fiancée.

Death has lessons for us, so it's up to us to dig down deep inside ourselves to find them. Each person who comes into our life has something to teach us, be it positive or negative. It's up to us to figure out what that lesson is. Even if the relationship is not a good one, there is a reason that person came into your life.

Looking back, the lesson I took from Bernie's death was that I had to let go. I had to let go of the anger that was still very much alive inside me from the tough times we had as husband and wife. But that doesn't mean I completely erased Bernie from my memory. I will never really let go of him. He will always be in my heart.

THREE

Finding My Path

With Bernie gone forever, I realized I had to do some soul-searching to find out what I was going to do with my life. Because Bernie and I were never officially divorced, as his widow I was able to collect his social security check every month. It was a big help because I had no one around who would help me and my three children. The Bards did nothing for us, and had nothing to do with us. These were their grandchildren, and they were just going to let them starve. As for my parents, my father had remarried, and his new wife cut him off from us. My mother, meanwhile, was living in her own little dreamworld, and she wanted us to have no part in it.

But I've always believed that we need to make the most of the cards we're dealt in life. And you never know when that winning hand is going to come up. Unfortunately, the next card I was dealt, Marvin Herman, was no King of Hearts. He was more like the joker. But, believe me, life with Marvin was no joke.

When I first met Marvin, I thought I had finally found not only the man of my dreams but the person who was going to make me famous. He was an accomplished songwriter who had worked with some big-name entertainers, and he had a few hit records. He was literally music to my ears, seeing how I was still under the illusion that I had what it took to make it as a singer. I was sure Marvin would launch my career. He had written songs for Elvis Presley, and he had managed Harold Melvin and the Blue Notes, so I thought stardom was just around the corner. Besides, he seemed to have a good head on his shoulders, and he appeared to be very well-off financially. But the truth was he wasn't very stable at all, and I would soon find out that he didn't have a dime to his name. Even though he had several hit records to his credit, he stupidly had sold the songs outright to the artists, never seeing any royalties when those songs became huge hits.

I first fell in love with Marvin's dreamy eyes. Little did I know that the dreaminess was caused by the thyroxine he needed to take to control his schizophrenic behavior! You would have thought I would have had some sort of premonition of impending trouble. But, no, love is blind, as they say. My eyes were *so* closed to what was going on around me.

Marvin had not had an easy life. His father was an abusive, very cruel man. He had a wooden arm that he would take off to beat Marvin with. He even cut off one of Marvin's fingers when he slammed a door on it. Such abuse no doubt contributed to Marvin's mental instability.

Crazy as he was, Marvin was also quite the character. He could charm the peaches right off the tree. And he really laid it on thick when he met me, telling me what a big shot he was in the music business, and then telling me exactly what I wanted to hear most: that I was going to be "a big singing star" someday. And I *so* believed him. To me, it was fate that we met.

While Marvin was a great songwriter, he wasn't so great as a manager. He had all of these grand ideas, but nothing ever came of them. He would audition acts, telling them how all of these music industry bigs were coming to his shows, then he would give these aspiring singers the "opportunity" to buy their way into the show. So all these hopefuls would get suckered into paying to be in his variety shows. Thinking Marvin was the man who was going to give them their lucky break, they eagerly handed over their money. He totally convinced them, like me, that they were going to be the next big thing.

But none of us ever went anywhere. The real show was going on behind the scenes, not up on the stage. All the talk about big-time talent agents in the audience wasn't true: Marvin padded the audience with his friends, none of whom were in the business. And when he couldn't fill the hall, he asked me to invite my friends and family. My sister Arlene and a whole crew of family members would come, and I would pay for all of the hamburgers they would eat after the show. I ended up losing money every time. This lack of money would seem to be the lesson I was supposed to be learning in life because I never seemed to have any. Anyway, I really don't know who was crazier: Marvin or me for going along with him.

Although Marvin generally was one big recipe for disaster, I have to admit he was a funny guy. If nothing else, he gave me the self-confidence to get up on stage and really sell a song. He told me how wonderful I was, and I believed him. Besides my grandmother Hattie, he was the only other person in my life who ever said anything positive like that to me. He also said something that has stayed with me all these years: "As long as you can look yourself in the mirror and know that you are a good person, and that you didn't hurt anybody in your life but yourself, you have to be proud of yourself." He also used to say, "You've got to know you are a good human being, and, if you are, things have got to turn your way eventually."

I've tried to live by those words my entire life. No matter what my circumstances—whether on the street homeless or living in a fancy Manhattan apartment and mingling with celebrity clientele—I have always tried to be a good person and make sure that I treat everyone with respect and compassion. We're all human beings, after all.

I hate it when people say about the homeless, "I never give them anything—they'll just spend it on booze or drugs anyway." I always tell them they shouldn't care what the homeless do with the money; that's their karma. People only should be concerned with their own karma. That homeless person may have crossed your path for a reason. Maybe this person has a lesson to teach you. And remember, it could happen to you: you could find yourself homeless one day. As you judge, so you will be judged. Helping out someone who's down on his luck, no matter how he got there, will go a long way.

Marvin was right. Be a good human being and things will eventually go your way. It took quite a while for things to go my way, however, especially with Marvin making all the decisions in my life. His half-baked schemes usually left us broke. But he was a good soul. We would have no money, barely making the rent, barely able to feed the kids and ourselves. But even during the most miserable of times he would hold me in his arms, rocking me to sleep while singing me one of his songs. I didn't care what happened then, as long as I was in his arms. I was that nuts about him.

Things went from bad to worse, however, and eventually we were in such bad shape financially that we were thrown out of our apartment with nowhere to go. We wound up staying with Marvin's mother in Queens. My older son, Michael, was in the navy by now, so I had only Melody and Ronnie with me. Marvin's mother wouldn't give us a key to the place because she felt that he was irresponsible and would leave the door unlocked. Sometimes she wouldn't hear us ringing the bell, however, so all four of us would camp out on the steps for the night. It kills me thinking about those nights, my children having no place to sleep.

My life was one big mess. I had no home, no income, no routine, and no promise of anything changing any time soon. No one cared what happened to my children or me. And even though Marvin was crazy and didn't have a cent to his name, I stayed with him anyway. I loved him, and his music, and his attitude that everything would be all right in the end. But the truth of the matter was that the only stable person in the house was Marvin's mother, and she was ninety years old and half deaf!

In 1978, I actually married Marvin. I don't know *what* I was thinking at the time. For all the good, he still was a ticking time bomb waiting to go off. Everything would be fine, then suddenly he would have one of his episodes, and the dark side of his personality would emerge. I can't count the times I took him to Bellevue Hospital, the times tears filled my eyes as they took him away in a straitjacket.

Most devastating of all was when Marvin was taken away and the children and I had no money and no place to go. Marvin used to carry around this fake wooden gun, and one night he came after me in the street with it. Some passing stranger must have called the police and Marvin was arrested. The police took him away, and my kids and I had nowhere to go. Marvin's mother wouldn't let us stay in her house without her son, so we were left to wander until he got out. It was bad enough for me to live this way; my children should not have had to.

Looking back on this period of my life makes me sick. It was the beginning of the end for us as a family. I lost touch with Ronnie, finding out later from my sister Arlene that he had enlisted in the service like his brother Michael because he couldn't take life on the street anymore. I knew then it was time to get my daughter off the street, so I called up my brother Alan and had him pick her up. He took Melody to live with my sister in Mount Vernon. While it broke my heart sending Melody away like that, I didn't want her living such a hard life.

When my family fell apart, my whole world fell apart. It was heartbreaking having everybody and everything taken away. I spent a lot of time in church, one of the few places I could feel somewhat safe. I also thought I could find some answers there. I would sit in front of the statues of Christ and the saints, asking, "Why are You doing this to me? How did I end up here?"

I thought it couldn't get much worse. I was living on the street and sleeping in the gutter. I was at the end of my rope and felt hopeless. I just wanted to lie down and die right then and there. I wasn't really living. I was existing.

As horrible as it was, my time on the street taught me many lessons, lessons I needed to learn. I learned that sometimes life doesn't turn out like you expect, and the only thing you can do is try to make it day by day. I learned to be grateful for what I have. I learned to be compassionate. And I learned that I was one tough cookie. For all I had been through, I survived.

I still have a cardboard box that I saved from that time. It's filled with pennies I begged for on the street. Also, there is a Polaroid snapshot of Marvin and me, one of Marvin's datebooks filled with notes and numbers, and my tiny Saint Jude statue, which I carried at all times for protection. The box reminds me where I came from. And whenever I'm in a rotten mood, it reminds me to be grateful for all I have.

One of the worst things that I learned from all this travail was how cruel people can be when you are homeless. People don't just give you a few pennies and then walk on. Some feel they have to say something horrible, and some even spit at you. "You dirty bitch," some would taunt, "why don't you get a job?"

It's not that easy to get a job when you are homeless. Where are you going to wash? Where are you going to get nice clothes for the interview? And who's even going to grant you an interview in the first place? Your only concern is finding food and shelter for that day, and you can't get either without money. And unless you beg, you can't get money without a job. It's a vicious cycle.

What's the point of harassing people who are down on their

luck? We're all human. If you're fortunate enough to have enough to eat and a roof over your head, thank God, then reach out to help someone who doesn't have those things.

Unfortunately, my situation got worse before it got better. While Marvin was a patient at a hospital in Queens, I would visit him for as long as they would let me stay. Some nights, I even slept in the lobby so I could visit him again first thing in the morning. Plus, I felt safe there. How wrong I was.

Late one night, I had to go to the bathroom, so I went into the ladies' room in the lobby. A man walked in right behind me, and then he viciously attacked me. He pushed me into one of the stalls, repeatedly banging my head against the wall, then he bent me over the toilet, shoved my head in the bowl, and raped me anally. When the animal was done, he left me there for dead, bruised and bleeding.

I somehow managed to pick myself up and make my way to the emergency room. But no one there would help me. All they did was treat me for hysteria, then send me on my way.

Crazy as it sounds, I returned to the hospital the next day to ask Marvin what I was supposed to do until he got out. Yes, I was consulting a man who was certifiably out of his mind, but, frankly, I had so few options, so few people in my corner. Marvin told me about a shelter in Times Square. So I took the subway to Manhattan—jumping the turnstile, of course—hoping to find a place to sleep.

On my way to the shelter, I passed Magnifique, a store selling crystals, mystic jewelry, and other things psychic. Even though I didn't have a dime to my name, I went in. I don't know why but I was drawn in.

Browsing through the store, I spotted a ring in a glass display case. It caught my eye not only because of its unique shape but also because it was turquoise, my favorite color. I asked the saleswoman to see it, and as I was looking at it I heard a man's voice behind me say, "That's for you, Yolana."

Now, at first I didn't pay any attention to the man because I had no idea he was talking to me because I was still going by the name Diane. But when the man repeated himself, I turned around and asked, "Who's Yolana?"

He said I was, and that that ring was for me. Then he paid the shopkeeper for the ring, said, "I'll see you again," and walked out of the store. Yet that wasn't the end of it. When I slipped the ring on my finger, a face appeared in the stone. Then the shopkeeper said, "You are going to make your mother's name famous."

My mother's name was Yolana, so it was odd coming out of nowhere like that. What made it even odder, however, was that it repeated what Lala Nanie and Juju Nanie had prophesized years before: that I was going to be famous, and that I was going to assume my mom's name. At the time, I chalked it up to coincidence. But eventually, it turned out to be true.

I finally made it to the shelter, but the place was a nightmare. I felt uneasy as soon as I walked in the door. I was given a cot to sleep on, but instead of feeling relieved I felt horrified. I was surrounded by drunks. They would get up in the middle of the night, laughing uncontrollably like lunatics for no reason. I thought if I stayed there, I would become a lunatic, too.

The more I tried to calm myself down, the louder the laughing grew, until my heart was racing. At the same time, my psychic abilities were opening up, and I could hear the growls of the bitter, angry souls that lived—and probably had died—there. The shelter was possessed, and I was tormented throughout the night by the living and the dead—not to mention the cockroaches and the rats. It was worse than the street!

So I jumped off my cot and ran out of there as fast as I could—so fast that I forgot my bag and shoes. I ran along Eighth Avenue barefoot until I reached a police station. Frazzled, with no shoes, no money, I must have been a sight to behold. I asked the officer at the front desk to help me out.

"Here's a dime. Now get lost," was all he said, throwing me a coin.

I took the dime to the nearest phone booth and I called my sister Arlene. I begged her to come get me, and, thankfully, she did. I wasn't asking her to let me live with her, I just didn't want to go back to that shelter.

Little did I know that she wasn't coming alone. She showed up with both my sons. Michael was stationed at Fort Totten, in Queens, and Ronnie just happened to be on leave visiting him when Arlene asked them to go with her to pick me up. I'll never forgive her for letting them see me when I was at my lowest. How could she do that to me? It was one of the most horrific moments of my entire life. I couldn't even look my kids in the eyes.

They took me to Grasslands Hospital in Westchester that very night. I was convinced that I was going to die there. All I could think was, this was going to be the last image my sons would have of their mother: thirty-eight years old and my life in shambles.

But my stay at Grasslands really helped me get back on my feet. I had my own room, where I slept on a mattress on the floor. But I was just grateful to be somewhere clean and safe. Nobody bothered me there. And, in fact, for the first time in my life people took care of *me*.

I stayed at Grasslands for a week, and I dreaded my release. I never wanted to leave. I thought Grasslands was my solution to homelessness. I thought it was God's plan for me to be safe. Little did I know He had other things in mind.

The staff at Grasslands found me a place to live, at the YWCA in South Yonkers. I had my own room there, and could come and go as I pleased, wandering around during the day, coming back at night. With no money, no job, what else was I going to do? I didn't even have enough money to pay for train fare so I could visit Marvin in the hospital in Queens. I was just waiting for his release so we could get our lives back.

It was hard for me to be alone on Mother's Day that year, and for the first and only time in my life I actually considered suicide. It wouldn't take all that much to just jump off that building and end it all, I'd say to myself, looking at some tall building. But then I'd think, what would my life mean if I did that? It would all have been for nothing. I still believed that there had to be a reason for me to be here, for me to go through all the crap I was going through.

Every day, I would go to church and curse at the crucifix hanging behind the altar. "I don't know what I am supposed to be doing!" I would shout. "I'm suffering!" I blamed God for all the misery in my life.

Then one day, while I was screaming, the cross lit up right before my eyes. I immediately dropped to my knees. "You have a gift," a voice told me, "now use it."

I looked around but was alone in the church. Then, looking at the base of the cross, I spied a playing card. Picking it up and turning it over, I saw it was the King of Hearts. The King of Hearts represents Christ.

It was then that my new life began. All my life, signs have presented themselves in my path to show me the way. Finding the King of Hearts was finding God. The voice I heard was God's. But I wasn't sure what the message was. From that point forward nonetheless, I became convinced God had a plan for me.

I started becoming much more psychic then, able to tune in to the voices I was hearing in my head. "Hearing" may be a misleading term. I was not detecting voices with my ears; the voices were in my head. Yet I knew I wasn't going crazy, that I wasn't experiencing schizophrenic delusions. My perceptions became much more acute overall. When one's psychic abilities open up, all the senses are heightened. You see more accurately, you hear more clearly, you smell more acutely. My experience in church that day not only let me know I had a purpose, it opened me up psychically and put me on the path to fulfill that purpose. Only I didn't know it yet.

Marvin eventually was released from the hospital, and it wasn't long before he cooked up one of his schemes. A wealthy woman needed a butler and a maid, a friend told him, and the friend had recommended the two of us. Who knows what he said that sold the woman on us. We certainly didn't have any experience. But we were desperate, so we would do anything to earn money and stay off the street.

The woman's name was Christina. She lived in a penthouse apartment on Madison Avenue with huge rooms and lots of windows. Christina was very beautiful, and we found out later that she was a princess or countess or something. But none of that mattered at the time—she could have been Countess Dracula. All we cared about was getting paid.

As the maid, I made beds, dusted, and emptied the litter box. The straightening up and cleaning part I didn't mind, but cleaning up after those two cats made me sick every time. To get out of it, I told Christina I was pregnant and couldn't empty the box. But it became obvious soon enough that I wasn't pregnant, yet she let me off the hook, doing it herself. Most people in her position would have fired a maid for refusing to do something, but she enjoyed my company, enjoyed talking with me. And I always enjoyed talking with her.

One particular day, Christina, in a rush, said to me, "I can't talk now. I'm going to be late for a reading." Having no idea what she was talking about, I asked, "What's a reading?" She told me she paid someone to read her cards and tell her fortune. "Don't go," I said. "I can do that for you—for free. I've been doing it all my life."

And that is how it all began. I read her cards, and blew her away with what I told her about her future. I wasn't looking to make a career out of reading cards at the time; I just wanted to do something for Christina because she had been so nice to Marvin and me. In fact, I was still dreaming of that career as a singer, with Marvin as manager. Besides, I thought anybody could read cards, that it was not so unusual.

I read Christina's cards every day after that. She stopped seeing other psychics. And I started my new life.

"I know Hans Holzer," Christina announced some time later, like it should mean something to me.

"Who is Hans Holzer?" I asked.

Christina explained that Holzer was revered as a master in the field of parapsychology and was the author of dozens of books on the subject. He was considered the psychic's psychic, and at the New York Institute of the Paranormal had taught innumerable people with psychic powers how to tap into and hone their skills. Intrigued, I hoped Christina would introduce me to him one day.

My wish came true right away. Christina said she was raving about me to Holzer, and that *he* wanted to meet me, so she had made an appointment for me to go see him. I was so nervous when I met him—petrified, is more like it. Why did this smart, important man want to meet me? I was such a jumble of nerves that I made Marvin come to the appointment with me.

When Hans Holzer answered the door, my first impression was that he was very proper. He had on an expensive suit, was clean-shaven, was very businesslike. His living room was full of books, statues, artifacts, and crystals. Marvin was really impressed, so impressed that he started picking things up and looking at them. I was embarrassed, and afraid he would break something. You just don't handle a stranger's possessions like that, especially when that stranger is Hans Holzer. But Marvin couldn't stop himself.

So right off the bat Marvin didn't make a good first impression. I could tell by the look in Holzer's eyes that he hated Marvin immediately. I would find out later that Holzer instinctively knew Marvin was not only bad news for me but also insane.

Holzer took me into his den shortly. We talked a bit; then he said he wanted to test me. He asked me to do a reading of him, his wife, his children, and his business. Not exactly sure what he meant, I went ahead and concentrated, trying to listen to what I heard inside my head, trying to see what I saw with my mind's eye. I started getting names and images, and when I told Hans about it he confirmed everything. I impressed him enough that he said he wanted to work with me.

Ultimately, Hans Holzer was a big help to me. He really launched me as a psychic. He showed me how to sharpen my perception; he gave me confidence in my abilities. He was also very demanding. If he said to be somewhere at six-thirty, he meant six-thirty, and if I wasn't there on the dot I wasn't allowed in. "Don't think you can be the prima donna," he would admonish me, "and just come in here when you want to. It doesn't work that way. You are going to do what I tell you to do or you are not going to make it." As severe as that sounds, he only wanted me to develop a strong work ethic, especially since I was just starting out.

Hans let me know that Marvin was no good for my career, that he didn't want me with Marvin at all. Get him out of your life, he told me. He was right, but I didn't listen at the time.

It was an honor to be working with Hans Holzer, yet I wasn't totally convinced that being a psychic was what I wanted to do with my life. I still wanted to be a singer.

But, in time, I realized I wanted to be a psychic full-time. Hans took me all over to do readings for the rich and famous, and I came to see that I really was good at it. I knew that if I was trained and polished by Holzer, that he would put me on the right track as a psychic.

I soon started making quite a nice living doing readings. And all along, Holzer made me a better psychic, tutoring me, testing my predictions. But he didn't train me to do readings only; he also involved me in past-life readings and even exorcisms. He broadened my horizons.

There was a statue of a lion outside of Holzer's apartment building that, on my way in, I would rub and then make a wish. "Come on, bring me some luck today," I would implore, and after a while I noticed that some of the wishes were coming true. It's Hans who really helped make them come true. And I listened to and hung on to his every word. Except about Marvin.

Instead of getting rid of Marvin, I made him my business manager. He was so good at getting money out of people, I reasoned, no doubt he would be good at lining up clients for readings. I totally blocked out the part about Marvin's inability to manage money, let alone his being insane.

But soon Marvin became one of the demons that I had to expel from my life. I couldn't let him drag me down with him. I had to choose between a crazy life with Marvin or a new life without him where I would be responsible for myself. True, Marvin introduced me to Christina, who introduced me to Hans, and that led to my calling. But I knew he would eventually be my downfall. I believe at some point in our lives, we all have to choose our own paths and take control of our lives. We must fight our own fights and live out our own destinies.

Everything in life happens for a reason; there are no coincidences. We all have many lessons to learn. Sometimes, I scratch my head and don't understand what's going on, yet I know it's all part of the master plan. I have a purpose. Everything that happened to me happened for a reason. Seeing the devil was a warning. If I had continued drinking, surely I would have met with trouble, because when you drink or do drugs your energy field is lowered and you become vulnerable to possession. If I hadn't stopped drinking, I believe, I almost certainly would have become possessed.

I had to learn who I was *not* before I could learn who I was. I had to battle the demons in my life to find my calling. And, let me tell you, it wasn't easy. But then, no one said life was supposed to be easy. It's just one big learning experience, and sometimes we have to learn lessons the hard way. But, sooner or later, if we pay attention, our life's purpose is made clear to us.

FOUR

Choosing
Your Destiny

I don't know if we each have a destiny, or if
we're all just floatin' around accidental-like
on a breeze. But I, I think maybe it's both.

—Forrest Gump

*A*lthough it's good to have people in your corner to help you make the big decisions in life, in the end you have to control your own destiny, make your own decisions. People can help you stay the course, but where you end up when the journey is over is your own doing.

Take my career as a psychic medium, for instance. Once requests for readings started rolling in, Marvin gave up writing songs to devote all of his time to my new livelihood. He started booking me for parties, where I would do individual readings for ten to fifteen dollars each. I was very accurate, and the word started to get out. And I was making good money, so Marvin and I moved into a studio apartment of our own in Sunnyside, Queens. It was about ten minutes from there to Manhattan, so I could easily get to the readings Christina and Hans booked for me. They put me in touch with the rich and famous, who became regular clients. I got other clients from renowned astrologer Lynn Palmer, who became a good friend. Lynn was and is known as the best astrologer in the world, and her clients were constantly asking her if she knew someone who did psychic readings. She would always give them my name.

My career started snowballing from there. One client recommended me to another, and another, and all of a sudden I had a full roster of regular clients who would come to me for spiritual advice. Marvin seemed to be on the phone morning, noon, and night booking appointments. He was a fine business manager for a while, but then he went off again, becoming jealous, and throwing fits. It caused major problems with my clients.

If I read for a man, Marvin accused me of sleeping with the client. He would follow me to readings, threatening both me and the client. Most of the men were terrified of him, as well as some of the women. One client ran out of her own apartment without her shoes after one of his tirades.

After witnessing this type of behavior time and again, even *I* feared for my safety. Although still in love with Marvin, I realized I had to get away from him. And I knew I couldn't succeed with him as my manager. Hans and Christina kept introducing me to influential people and Marvin kept driving them away.

I wish I had listened to Hans when he first told me to break away from Marvin. It would have saved me so much aggravation and heartache. I believe Marvin had my best interests at heart. And I believe he couldn't help it if he was insane. But seeing him get closer and closer to the edge was frightening. I just couldn't bear seeing him committed again.

Still, my career was taking off like a rocket. Hans got my name out to anyone and everyone he knew. He also wrote a story about me for *The Enquirer,* and the feedback was tremendous. They received bagfuls of mail from people wanting to know about the future. They forwarded the letters to Hans, who then would forward them to me.

The letters not only contained questions but cash—two dollars, five dollars, whatever the correspondent could spare—and self-addressed, stamped envelopes, so I could respond as soon as possible. I would do readings during the day, then tackle the mailbag at night. Things were looking up for me.

As fate would have it, however, I couldn't have success without getting a dose of misfortune along with it. My sister told me that our mother had been diagnosed with cancer and wasn't doing well. My mother and I had been estranged for years, with her living in Connecticut near my sister and brother, and I hadn't had much contact with her. I went to see her in the hospital, hoping we could reconcile our differences somehow, but it just wasn't meant to be. She long ago had written me out of her life, and wanted nothing to do with me.

Nonetheless, when she died I attended the funeral. Hans advised against it. "No, you don't have to go," he said. "There's nothing there but a body." To dissuade me from going, he booked a reading that day. But I went anyway, after the reading.

Two friends of mine, both psychologists, accompanied me. When we drove up to the funeral parlor, my family was standing around outside—my sister, my brother, all of them—and they were looking at me like I had no right to be there, like I had done something wrong to my mother.

I hadn't done anything to Mother. I was there to pay my respects. One of my friends, noticing the chilly welcome, turned to me and said, "You can do one of two things. You can be the scapegoat and go in there and take more abuse. Or you can walk away. You don't need this. You don't deserve this. Know you have choices."

As my friend was telling me all this, I looked over to my sister and brother, who turned away immediately and did their very best to ignore me. Not feeling like being a martyr, I made my choice and walked away. I had only wanted to pay my respects to the woman who brought me into this world, but it didn't work out that way. It was really a sad day.

I learned a valuable lesson because of that funeral: I don't have to do anything I don't want to, and I have choices. I am in control of my own outcome, no one else.

Every day, we face circumstances not of our own making. We have options and the path we choose determines our destiny. Forrest Gump was right. Yes, we all have a destiny, but we can control the path getting there.

By staying with Marvin, I chose the path I had to follow.

Marvin was not only causing problems with my clients by then, he also was booking me in some crazy places. For instance, he booked me at a Manhattan bar. One of the owners had told Marvin the bar was haunted, and asked if I could come in, tap into the spirit that was possessing the place, and get rid of it. Contacting a ghost, let alone exorcism, was something that I had never attempted before, but Marvin agreed, and negotiated a fee, without knowing what he was getting me into.

I wasn't fully aware of the scope of my powers at the time and didn't know if I could do what they wanted. I went in blind but soon found out I was in way over my head.

Melody, my twelve-year-old daughter, who was still living with my sister, came along for the ride. The bar was located in a building that dated back to the Revolutionary War. Another owner told us a man had hanged himself upstairs back then, and apparently everyone who worked there had seen or heard him at one time or another. Even the electricity was screwed up, with lights going on and off without warning. And things would move from one place to another without anyone touching them, or disappear altogether. Nobody liked being there alone after closing.

After hearing all this, Melody and I headed upstairs. I remember us going up together, but after that I draw a blank. Apparently, the craziness started as soon as we got up there. Melody says she was looking around and all seemed normal, but then, out of nowhere, a voice came out of my mouth that was not mine. When she asked me why I was pitching my voice so deeply, I wouldn't give her a straight answer. I just started laughing in a totally different voice. Melody thought it was the man who had hanged himself trying to communicate with her through me. She says by that point everything had changed about me, not only my voice, but my features as well.

By then, Melody had heard and seen enough, and she didn't hang around for more. She was scared to death, and, mother or no mother, she wasn't staying. She bolted out of the room, down the stairs, and out of the front door and right into the car. She wanted nothing to do with that unhappy dead man!

> *When Yolana is in a trance I have no doubt that the individuals speaking through her are indeed the people they claim to be and that Yolana has no knowledge of what is coming through her lips.* —HANS HOLZER

When I came out of my trance, I didn't know where I was. My heart was pounding, and I was terrified. Once I got my bearings, I ran downstairs and out of the building.

Melody told me what had happened, and I called Hans right away to tell him. He was sure the spirit had possessed me. Spirits can tap into a person's energy, and, boy, this spirit tapped into mine. It took complete control of me, and tried to communicate through me. It used me like a telephone.

I found out later that this spirit was what is known as a "lowly evolved spirit." This type of spirit is often animal-like and evil. Connecting with such a spirit even today can get me in over my head. I could have physical problems, like not being able to breathe, or experiencing a sudden drop in blood pressure. That's why I need someone like Hans to guide me to keep me safe.

There are also "highly evolved spirits," which stay on this plane because they need to communicate some sort of message. For instance, when I do a simple reading the spirits of the dead may come through me, and they are considered highly evolved. Maybe it's the spirit of a child who wants to tell his mother not to cry for him anymore, that he's okay. It's entirely different than communicating with a lowly evolved spirit. Me contacting your dead grandmother isn't going to harm me physically.

Haunting and possessions are a whole different ball game.

They can make me violently sick if there isn't someone around, such as a parapsychologist, who understands what I have tapped into, who knows how to communicate with and "exit" the entity from my body.

So Marvin's booking me to work in haunted places didn't do anybody any good. The people who hired me didn't get the problem solved; the spirit didn't get put to rest; and I certainly didn't get any laughs out of it. I needed to exorcise Marvin from my life in order to take control of my destiny and become the psychic and person I was put on this earth to be.

However, before I got Marvin out of my life there would be a few more adventures. I still loved him, and I still thought I could get him help.

One of the last times I tried to get Marvin some help, I decided he needed to go to Grasslands, the place that put me back on my feet. I called my son Ronnie, who had just gotten out of the army, and told him that Marvin was sliding into one of his schizophrenic episodes and needed treatment.

Ronnie agreed to take Marvin to Grasslands. He drove to Queens, picked Marvin up, and drove him away.

On the way to Grasslands, Marvin was looking at the license plates, saying things like, "That guy doesn't know that I know he's a federal officer. The prefix on his license plate is 892, so I know he's a fed." He also pulled a switchblade on Ronnie, then started pointing it at people in other cars and waving his hands frantically. Luckily, Ron somehow talked him into putting the knife away. When they got to Grasslands, he asked Marvin for it. He put it in his back pocket for safekeeping.

Ronnie took Marvin to reception, where a nurse helped check

Marvin in. She took Marvin to be examined, and a little while later a doctor appeared to speak with Ronnie in private.

The doctor started asking him a number of questions, like *he* was the patient. Before he knew it, she told him they had released Marvin and that they were going to admit *him*!

Trying to explain just how crazy Marvin was, Ron retrieved the switchblade from his back pocket, to show the doctor what Marvin had brandished in the car. The doctor, alarmed, pressed the panic button connecting the room to the nurses' station.

Before Ronnie knew it, he was being restrained. Marvin had turned the tables on Ronnie, who had to have Grasslands contact me to vouch for him, releasing him when I did.

Ronnie, reunited with Marvin, had no intention of taking Marvin back home to me. Instead, he took him to the nearest train station, putting him on the first train headed anywhere. Ronnie didn't care where, he just wanted Marvin on it and out of my life.

It wasn't easy getting Marvin on that train—he didn't want to go alone. Ronnie gave him a key chain with miniature dollar bills on it, and said, "Here. Take this. This will protect you." It was enough to calm Marvin down, apparently, and he boarded the train.

The incident at Grasslands wasn't the end of it, however. Marvin eventually found his way back to Queens, and, of course, I took him back in. His life seemed like one roller-coaster ride after another, with me strapped in the seat next to him, never knowing what to expect next. With Marvin, it was either some wacky deal or some big crisis. I was getting to the point where I couldn't deal with it anymore.

It is really awful when you love someone who is that sick, that self-destructive. But I had to have my own life without Marvin showing up all the time and ruining it for me. I hated the thought of saying good-bye yet I knew I had to. I just didn't know how.

That's when God intervened and sent me an angel. While God is always with me, He has an uncanny knack for showing up at the eleventh hour and rescuing me. After all I've been through, I know this firsthand: God is always around us and He is good.

The angel God sent was Herb Michaelson, a psychologist who I met through Hans Holzer. We hit it off right off the bat and quickly became friends.

I told Herb what was going on between Marvin and me. I told him about the way Marvin acted whenever I would give people readings—especially men—and right away Herb expressed concern for my safety. He told me Marvin's personality type knew no boundaries, that he should be under a doctor's care and probably on medication. Herb, like Hans, advised me to leave Marvin, but, again, I just couldn't do it. That is, until one night when I had to leave or be killed.

Marvin and I had just returned home from a reading in Manhattan, and as soon as we walked in the door he lost it. He told me he knew I was a werewolf, and that he had a silver bullet and that he was going to kill me with it. He went into the bedroom and came back with a gun.

Terrified, I ran out of the apartment without my coat or pocketbook. I feared for my life. I had no idea if the gun was loaded—or if he even had the silver bullet he was talking about. All I knew was that I had a gun pointed at my head and I didn't want to die.

I ran to a store around the block and asked to use the phone, to call Herb. He was home, thank God, and he told me to stay put, that he would come pick me up. He took me to his girlfriend's house, where I stayed for the next week.

Herb then came up with the solution that would keep Marvin out of my life for good: moving to a women's hotel where no men are allowed. He knew of one, the Martha Washington Hotel, just off of Madison Avenue at Twenty-sixth Street. He made all the arrangements, even lending me the money to get started since everything I owned was with Marvin in Sunnyside.

It was the best move I ever made.

Without Marvin in my life, I was able to focus on my work, and on me. The Martha Washington's rules keeping him at bay, I was able to do my readings uninterrupted.

I began reading for women at the hotel for free just to get back in the swing of things. If they liked what I told them, I figured, they would come back for more. And they would tell their friends. Their word of mouth would attract new clients.

My life has had its ups and downs and taken many twists and turns. Looking back now, I realize it was all the result of the choices I made. Do I wish I had done things differently? Sure I do. I wish I could have avoided all the heartache, all the sorrow. But I also know that all along I was in charge of my destiny and the choices I made taught me invaluable lessons, and brought me to the place I am today.

FIVE

*From the
Nuthouse
to the
Penthouse*

Within a matter of months after moving into the Martha Washington Hotel, I had a full roster of clients, which allowed me to pay my own way for the first time in my life. It had taken until the mid-1980s, but I finally had a roof over my head that wasn't my parents', my husband's, or a shelter's or an institution's, and I was starting to feel good about myself. I had just gone from living on the streets unable to take care of my children, let alone myself, to living on my own and helping others.

I read for my female clients in my room, and for my male clients at the Weathervane Restaurant or the Metropolitan Coffee Shop across the street. But my room wasn't always the best venue for readings because I always had "visitors"—not people, or even spirits or ghosts, but the creepy crawly kind. I would be giving a reading to some poor woman when, out of nowhere, a gigantic cockroach would emerge from under the bed. I would try to squash the intruder nonchalantly before the client laid eyes on it, hoping my movements would blend in with the twisting and turning that my body goes through when picking up messages from the other side. And usually the client was so focused on what I was saying that she didn't even notice I was stomping a bug before her very eyes anyhow. I not only was contacting the spirit world, I was contacting the insect world. In truth, I may have been as good an exterminator as a psychic back then. I was my own "roach motel."

When not conducting readings, I honed my skills with Hans Holzer. Impressed with my progress, he introduced me to a number of well-known, rich individuals. In no time, they became regular clients. I would read for them in their posh offices, ritzy apartments, or luxurious hotel suites, advising them on important issues affecting their lives. In what seemed the blink of an eye, I went from the nuthouse to the penthouse. Before, I couldn't run my own life; now I was telling bigwigs how to run theirs.

It just goes to show that you should never give up on your dream because it could be just around the corner. I had gone from surviving on the streets of New York, where people were rude and crude, to earning a living in some of the city's most expensive penthouses—where some of the people were even more rude and two times as crude. But I also came into contact with a few good eggs.

Lynn Palmer, for one. Hans Holzer introduced me to the great astrologer. He had asked her to line me up with some clients, and, without hesitation, she had done it. She really worked hard on my behalf. Because of her, and Hans, I was busy all the time.

One of the first celebrities whom Lynn recommended me to was Mickey Rooney. Well, it was a reading and a half. I read for him in his hotel room on the West Side, and I have to admit that I was woozy almost from the start. I had never met anyone as hyperactive as he.

Initially, I thought it was me. This was my first reading for a well-known star, after all, so I thought it was nerves that were making me feel dizzy. Then I realized it was Mickey who had my head spinning.

In person, Mickey Rooney is the same, highly animated person you see in the movies and on television. He is "on" all of the time, however. Not sitting still for a second, he paced from one side of the room to the other, on the phone constantly.

From one second to the next, I didn't know where he was going to be, making it almost impossible to give him an accurate reading. His hyperactive personality made it almost impossible to remember what I said to him a minute earlier. When I did get him to sit still, and told him things about his life, he didn't want to hear it. He didn't want my advice; he felt he knew it all already.

I had no idea how to deal with this type of personality. I had to admire Lynn for being able to deal with him. This man's hyper, I remember thinking to myself. I got so frustrated I almost walked out. Needless to say, the reading was a disaster.

It was the only time I met with Mickey Rooney, and, to be honest, I was relieved. I knew I would never be able to read for him. I wasn't ever going to be able to tap into all that extraneous energy.

Even though it wasn't the greatest experience, I was grateful to Lynn nonetheless for recommending me to Mickey. And it was just the beginning. She continued to recommend me to any number of high-profile types, including doctors, lawyers, business executives, diplomats, and celebrities—I read for them all. I was really coming into my own as a reader.

And I started dressing the part too. I have to admit, I was quite a sight back then. I had these long acrylic fingernails, fake eyelashes, and big teased-out blond hair. What had I been thinking? I got caught up in the whole Hollywood gypsy fortune-telling thing, I suppose. I guess if my readings didn't have an impression, certainly my "looks" did.

The nails, in fact, were quite the hit with reporters who wrote stories about me back then. Their features would always mention my "three-inch claws."

My telephone rang off the hook constantly now, with people from all walks of life wanting one-on-one readings. They either had been recommended by Hans or Lynn, or they had read about me in such magazine articles as Holzer's "Amazing Psychic Housewife," which appeared in *The Enquirer*. While most of them sought me out to help them change their lives, little did they know the huge role they played in helping me change my life.

One such client was the fashion designer Diane von Furstenberg. About a year after I had moved in to the Martha Washington, I received a call from a woman named Lillian who wouldn't reveal her last name. I could care less about her last name, all I cared about was whether she had the money to pay me. We set up an appointment for her to come over and as soon as she walked through the door, the name Diane popped into my head.

"Who's Diane?" was my first question.

Lillian told me that Diane was her daughter, but then she didn't let me focus on her, pulling photographs of other people out of her bag and asking me about them instead. I can't recall now who they were, or what I told her about them. All I remember is that the reading was good but uneventful. But the name Diane stayed with me, even after Lillian left.

Three months later, Diane's secretary called me to make an appointment for her boss. That's when I found out that Lillian's daughter was Diane von Furstenberg, then as now one of the top fashion designers in the world—and, at the time, married to Egon von Furstenberg, a prince, which made her a princess.

I recall going over to the von Furstenberg apartment like it was yesterday. Wearing a black skirt, black blouse, my hair tucked up under a black hat, I was so nervous visiting my first celebrity home. The apartment, like others in the building, occupied an entire floor. It was stunning, plush, and very intimidating.

A maid met me at the door, and soon Diane herself greeted me cordially. I wondered what I could possibly tell a women like this, as my shaking hand shook her steady one.

But then I gave myself a pep talk, telling myself that I was good at what I do, I should trust myself and get on with it. The worst that could happen would be that she wouldn't like what I had to say. It couldn't be worse than living on the street.

Looking back now, I think living on the street helped me deal with a lot of my insecurities over the years. Everything happens for a reason. Everything has a lesson to teach us.

Diane led me into the living room, where she stretched out comfortably on a couch like a queen——I was in the presence of royalty. Yet she couldn't have been nicer, not condescending in the least.

I began the reading by reciting names and events that were all familiar to her, people and things she had questions about. I told her about her past, her present, and her future, and she listened very receptively to everything with baited breath.

Then we talked about spirituality, past lives—things of that nature. Diane specifically wanted to know all about karma, and why I thought we were put on this earth.

All in all, we talked for about an hour and a half. When the reading was over, she generously paid me more than my usual fee, and she told me I'd be hearing from her again real soon. I couldn't wait to be invited back.

Diane von Furstenberg is not your typical celebrity. She doesn't think that she is superior to anyone, or that people owe her anything. And she certainly isn't looking to get anything for free. I mean, some celebrities must think they're doing you a favor by allowing you to read them. Not Diane. She treated me as an equal and she paid me well. As a matter of fact, she treated me as if *I* were the celebrity, even telling me I looked like Doris Day. I wanted to look like Ava Gardner, but Doris was good enough. In fact, it went straight to my head. If she thinks I look like Doris Day, I thought to myself, maybe I should revive that singing career! But then reality pulled my head out of the stars.

Diane also sent me clients regularly. Everyone at her company seemed to want my number, and she didn't hesitate to give it. She even recommended me to people she sat next to on airplanes, people she met on her travels.

I would see Diane herself every two to three weeks, and we

became very friendly. She was genuinely interested in me and how I was doing, and, before I knew it, she was inviting me to her lavish parties. I'd have to be almost forced to go because of my aversion to going out, but once I got there I'd have a great time. Everybody who was anybody was there, and Diane always made me feel comfortable.

Once she threw a party for Raquel Welch, and Jack Nicholson, Richard Gere, gossip columnist Liz Smith, and Andy Warhol were there. I got a kick out of Nicholson. Here was one of the biggest stars in Hollywood at a party not only with his peers but also the press and his suit was so wrinkled he looked like he just rolled out of bed in his pajamas. "What happened to your suit?" I asked him.

Without missing a beat, he looked me up and down and joked, "You should talk."

I was introduced to Liz Smith at another von Furstenberg party. She was intrigued when she found out I was a psychic, more so when she found out that Claus von Bulow was a client of mine. She asked me my thoughts on the case. I explained to her that the only thing he was guilty of was infidelity, and that if that were a crime then fifty percent of the American public should be locked up. His European suaveness worked against him, a coolness that Americans couldn't relate to and therefore distrusted.

Liz and I had a great time that night, and, to my surprise, the following item appeared in her column the next morning:

The other night at a party in the exotic apartment of Diane von Furstenberg I met a blond dynamic woman who was introduced simply as Yolana. It turns out that she is a psychic who has practiced her art of seeing into the future for such diverse persons as the designing princess who was our hostess and also for Claus von Bulow.

The rest of the column went on to recount the conversation we had about von Bulow. I couldn't believe I had made it into the newspaper, my name right there along with all those celebrities!

I had met Claus von Bulow after a reading for a client who had shown me his photograph and I had said he would be having very serious legal problems soon. The next thing I know, von Bulow called me for a reading.

I met von Bulow in the coffee shop across from the Martha Washington. When I saw him, I remember thinking how elegant he looked. I also remember I couldn't pronounce his name correctly. But he didn't seem to mind. He was very gracious about it, as a matter of fact, telling me you say it like "Santa Claus." He did use another name when he booked the appointment, however, since it was right before his first trial and no doubt he didn't want me to know who he was beforehand.

I gave him a reading, telling him that he was in for a very rough time. He began to cry, but not for himself. He felt badly that his daughter, Cosima, also had to go through this. He loved her more than anything in the world, and he never wanted to hurt her. But he didn't have to explain this to me. I also knew he hadn't killed his wife, Sunny, from the first minute I had seen his photograph.

I always felt that Claus von Bulow was not the type of man who would hurt a fly. I also felt he never would have consulted a psychic if he were guilty of killing his wife. I told him he would be found innocent when retried on appeal. When I told him this, his spirits lifted a bit.

I spoke with Claus periodically on the phone because I felt he needed a friend, and then he came back to see me before his second trial. It was at this reading that I advised him to hire a new lawyer, suggesting Alan Dershowitz. On June 10, 1985, with Dershowitz at his side, von Bulow was acquitted of all charges.

Another well-to-do individual who helped me out during my early years as a psychic was Susan Kasen. She was one of the main reasons I was able to move out of the Martha Washington and into the world of the rich and famous. I met her after giving her mother a reading, and she was fascinated by my ability. Little did I know that she not only would become one of my best clients but also a dear friend.

But Susan hated coming to the Martha Washington, and she hated even more that I had to live there. She always was telling me she was going to get me out of there if it was the last thing she did.

While Susan didn't have a lot of money, she was a real Martha Stewart type, everything she was involved in became successful, like her flower shop, which was financed by Ron Pearlman. When she offered me her Hamptons summerhouse, I declined, not having any idea how to live or act in a place like that. I would never be able to afford the lifestyle that went with the house. But Susan didn't see it that way. Money and class didn't matter to her. If she liked you, there wasn't a thing she wouldn't do for you.

Every time Susan came to the Martha Washington Hotel for a reading, she'd tell me, "You can't stay here. It is a dive. What are you doing here?"

In turn I would respond: "What am I doing here? What are you talking about? I'm lucky to have this roof over my head. I can't afford to go anywhere else. It costs money to get out of here, and I don't have any money. I'm lucky I can afford to live here."

"Don't worry about it," she reassured me, "I'll take care of it." And she did.

The next thing I knew, Susan did something that I'll never forget as long as I live. She made all the arrangements for me to move to an apartment in a building called the Plaza 50, paying the first six months' rent in advance. The Plaza 50 was uncharted territory for me, a big improvement in my living situation but also a big responsibility. On one hand, I was so grateful to Susan for doing this for me; on the other hand, I was scared to death of assuming the rent once those first six months were up. How am I going to do this? I used to sit up nights thinking to myself. But I had enough regular clients by then that I was able to manage.

It was Susan Kasen who really got me back on my feet again. She not only set me up in a nice apartment, she also invited me to her cocktail parties and introduced me to her inner circle. I never met a woman with more chutzpah. She could work a room like no one else.

On one occasion, one of Susan's guests was a very famous writer I will refer to as "Margo." She was there with her husband, "Boris," and when he found out I was a psychic, he wanted a free reading. But before I could read for Boris, Margo took me aside to warn me about what I should and should not tell him. "You better not tell him anything negative," she chided me, "or you're going to regret it."

Margo had some nerve telling me how to do my job. How would she like me telling her what to write? My heart was pounding. I was just starting to do business with some very wealthy and influential people, and if this very well-known writer ever wrote anything bad about me she could end my career before it even got started. I also knew I really couldn't monitor the information that would be coming through me. Most of the time, I don't even remember what I've said. So how was I going to hold back when in a trance? I had never had to censor myself before. Would it affect the accuracy of what I was about to tell Boris? If I couldn't say what I thought, what was I going to say?

As if this pressure weren't enough, then Margo suddenly can't find her pocketbook, and she immediately blames me. "Oh, the reader must have taken it."

Oh great, I thought. First this woman threatens me, then she accuses me of stealing. I had no idea what would happen next. The only thing I knew was that she was older than the hills, and her face was covered in more makeup than I had ever seen in my life. I almost suggested to Margo that she look under all that makeup for her purse, but I thought better of it. I was a guest of Susan's, and I owed it to her to be as nice as possible to Margo. Finally, one of the maids found the pocketbook upstairs.

I couldn't wait for the party to be over. I didn't want Boris or Margo, or any of these people, as clients. I didn't care how much money any of them had. They all seemed to be snobs, with Margo the biggest snob of all.

I didn't enjoy going to parties like those, but I knew I had to attend to meet new clients. At these parties I learned how *not* to treat people. And while all the rich and famous are not like Margo, she did give me an even greater appreciation of my own world—no matter how humble it was.

I saw firsthand how mean and selfish some rich people can be. That's why I'm no longer impressed by people with money. I learned money can't buy class.

On my journey from the nuthouse to the penthouse, I found out what being rich really was all about. No matter how much money you have, you are never truly rich if you don't make friends with your inner self. Your best friend is you.

SIX

*A
Little Help
from
My Friends*

As word got out that I was a good psychic, I became overwhelmed trying to manage my clients. I needed to hire a secretary, maybe two, to keep all my appointments straight. I also had no way of getting to appointments when clients wanted me to come to them. For a while, my oldest son Michael played chauffeur, but he was living on a military base in Brooklyn at the time, driving to the city to take me to readings, and I knew it couldn't last. So while things were taking off for me, they were also getting out of hand. I needed help, but where was I going to get it? So I turned to Christ, and again He answered my prayers.

Esther, my first assistant, showed up at my apartment one night for a reading. She had heard about me from her boyfriend, and when they started having problems in their relationship she sought me out. But we didn't exactly start off on the right foot.

Esther confided that she had expected me to be an old shawl-wearing hunchback with a heavy accent. But when she saw the fake fingernails, the fake eyelashes, and the big hair, she was quite skeptical. She thought I might be an out-of-work actress; no way was I a legitimate psychic. Little did she know that I could read her mind, and without so much as a hello I informed her, "You ain't no bed of roses yourself, sweatheart."

As much as my appearance put Esther off, her appearance put me off. She was wearing a trench coat, and I remember thinking, Who does she think she is, Inspector Clouseau? She strode in like some kind of detective, her skepticism obvious. I assured her I was legit, so what did it matter what I looked like? Besides, the reading cost only ten dollars. What did she think she was gonna get for ten dollars anyway? Dinner and a freakin' movie?

Esther and I sat down at my kitchen table, and I began the reading. But she was one tough cookie. She sat there in her coat, not the least interested or impressed by what I was telling her. But I ignored her, and battled her negative vibes. Staring right at her, I began to rattle off names.

Right away, I got her boyfriend's name, and I explained why she was having problems with him. To convince her that what I was saying was true, I named a couple of other people in her life, and told her things about them that only she knew.

When I finished the reading, I told Esther that this wasn't going to be the last we were going to see of one another. But she didn't believe that or anything else I told her. "You're outta your head, lady," she fired back in what I came to know as typical Esther fashion.

"Maybe I am," I answered, "but you'll see. Someday you'll work for me, and you're gonna say I was right about your boyfriend."

Sure enough, not long after that, the things I told Esther about her boyfriend started coming true, and she started calling me for comfort and advice. One night she was so upset she called me in hysterics, and I managed to calm her down. After that, she began calling me almost daily.

Esther patched things up with her boyfriend, and she even sent him in for a reading, but I never told her what I saw. For starters, any information I give to a client is confidential. If the client wants to discuss the reading, that's his or her choice. So when she asked me about her boyfriend's reading, I told her to ask him.

I had told her in her first reading that her boyfriend was no good for her, but she didn't believe me. As it turns out, she and he didn't last too long after that, and it was around then that I asked her if she wanted to come work for me. I told her that at the same time she would be helping me out, I would be helping her out, if only because she would have less free time to think about her cheating ex-boyfriend.

At first, Esther was hesitant to accept my offer, especially since she already had a full-time position as a high-level secretary, but then she agreed to juggle both jobs. She would work her day job from nine to five, then handle my phone messages and book appointments in the evenings.

Esther also was great at hustling me up more business, it turned out. She really knew how to put that big mouth of hers to work for me. Everywhere she went, she spread the word, handing out my card at beauty and nail salons, even on the subway. Whoever Esther came into contact with, she was sure to tell them all about me.

It was around this same time that I also met Josephine Sonnenblick, another important person in my life. I was booked to do a psychic party in Brooklyn, and as soon as I walked in the door I asked one of the ladies in the living room, "Where's Josephine?"

"She's not here," the poor woman said, turning white as a ghost. "She called and said she was tired."

"Bull," I said. "Your friend's too cheap to pay for a reading. Tell her to show up the next time I'm here."

Four months later, the same group of ladies booked me at the same house, and this time Josephine showed up. One of the first things I picked up on was that someone had just asked her to watch her language around me, so I immediately found the woman who said that to Jo and told her: "You have to stop being so uptight." And then I walked right up to Josephine, pretending I didn't know who she was, and said, "Where's Josephine? Did that cheap tramp come tonight?" I intuitively knew I could joke with her like that, that she had a great sense of humor.

Later, following this introduction, I noticed that Josephine had a plastic bag full of pocketbooks that she was selling. This certainly wasn't what I had in mind when it came to the person who would eventually become my secretary. I felt bad about saying she was too cheap to come to the first reading, and I thought maybe I had read her wrong: maybe she really didn't have the money. As a way of making amends, I bought whatever pocketbooks she had, even though I didn't need one.

When it came to her reading, Jo was as tough a customer as Esther. I asked to see the photographs she had with her, but nothing about her life jumped out at me. All I was getting were things related to her house. "You have a mice problem," I told her. "Some pipes need fixing, and your car needs repairs." But that was it. Nothing juicy.

Then I asked, "Who's Don?," and, to my surprise, she didn't know. I was really stumped, because I kept getting the name Don. She is either a really boring person, I was thinking to myself, or my psychic antennae needed adjusting.

"No wonder I didn't want to spend money on this reading the last time," Josephine suddenly announced, stunning me even more. "You didn't tell me anything exciting about my life or myself. I didn't pay thirty dollars to hear about my water pipes and my car."

"What can I tell a person with your life?" I barked back. "What's going on in your life that's so exciting? I don't see any excitement. As a matter of fact, I think you're boring."

I then asked what her husband's name was and when she answered Don, I nearly had a canary.

"You're so out of it you didn't even pick up when I said Don is important to you. How do you expect me to tell you anything about you when you can't even remember your husband's name?"

I went on to tell her that Don was a good-hearted soul, that she was living an excellent life because of him, and that's why nothing major was coming up. I told her she should be happy that all I was getting was mice and broken pipes, not cancer or death or any horrible things like that. I told her to appreciate her good fortune.

It seemed to go in one ear and out the other at the time. I mean, she wanted to hear that she would be running off with Robert Redford, and that she was going to be rich like the characters on *Dynasty,* when, in reality, her life was more *Brady Bunch* than anything else.

But even though we butted heads that first night, our relationship eventually blossomed into one of the best friendships I have ever had. After hearing me field her girlfriends' calls about things psychic, she started calling me herself. Inevitably, our conversations ended in big belly laughs. I kept begging her to come work for me, but she kept telling me she already had a job at an ice-cream factory. After a while, she gave in, and came on board part-time to start.

Josephine and Esther would take turns booking and driving me to appointments. I learned pretty quickly, though, that they meant more to me than just work. Yes, God sent them to me to help me, but I also believe He sent them to me to make me laugh. I can't tell you all the laughs I had with those two ladies. They were always fun to work with.

One time, Esther and I were leaving for a party in Brooklyn, and I mentioned that I was getting a vision that we were going to be in an accident on the way home. Well, she just lost it. "I'm quitting this job," she yelled. "I've never been afraid of anything in my life, but ever since I've been working for you too many crazy things happen. You've made me a wreck."

I then told her that I was seeing a blue car with a white top, so we decided we would take the subway home that night to avoid any possible accident with a car.

Wouldn't you know it, by the time the party was over we had missed our train. To top it off, it had started to snow.

As we were trying to figure out how to get home, a nice gentleman from the party offered to drive us into the city. But Esther hesitated. What color was his car? she wanted to know, and when he answered blue her chin almost hit the pavement. But when she asked him what color the top was and he said black, she was relieved. I was so exhausted from all the readings at the party that I had totally forgotten about my prediction about the accident.

So we got into the car, and just as we approached the Midtown Tunnel Esther asked the man to turn off to drop her off at her house. The snow was really coming down hard by this time, and I told her that we would be better off staying on the highway, that it would be a lot safer than the side streets.

Just as I was saying this, our car was rear-ended by another car with a loud bang. Esther landed on the backseat floor, her hat down over her eyes. I told the driver not to open his door because I believed another car was about to hit us. A few seconds later, it did, smacking into the rear passenger's door and again sending Esther flying. After that, I told them both that I felt it was over, that we were now okay.

"You bitch," Esther yelled at me, getting up into the seat and pulling her hat up. "You were right again!"

But little did she know that our troubles weren't over. The driver of the car that hit us on the left-hand side had opened his door and was bellowing that he was going to kill someone. I sensed immediately that he was on alcohol and drugs, and that he wasn't in his right mind.

Ignoring the outburst, our driver asked him for his license and insurance card numbers, which sent the lunatic over the edge. He picked up a piece of the metal fender that had fallen off one of the cars and starting threatening our driver with it.

"Holy shit, he's got a machete!" Esther screamed.

I knew that if I didn't do or say something quickly, this guy would hurt our driver, and possibly us, too. Esther, trying to help, screamed at the top of her lungs, but it only made matters worse. I quickly turned around and told her to be quiet. Then I saw that the enraged driver had our driver by his coat lapels. "Anthony," I commanded firmly, "leave him alone."

At the sound of his name, Anthony let go of our driver, then looked at me. Esther, completely silent, was obviously in shock. Our driver also seemed puzzled by my knowing the other driver's name, even though he knew I was a psychic.

Now that everyone was calmed down, I tried to get us help. "HELP!" I yelled, sticking my head out into the cold, snowy air. "HELP ME, SOMEONE! I'M HAVING A BABY!"

By this time, an ambulance had arrived on the scene. The EMT workers wanted to take all of us to the hospital for tests, and Esther threw a fit, telling them that she was okay, that she didn't need any doctor. But she stopped resisting when I told her that we had better go because the other driver's rage hadn't run its course. So the three of us climbed into the ambulance and went to the hospital. Once the doctors heard our story, and saw that we were all right, we were released.

Esther and I then took a cab to my apartment. She complained all the way, still angry with herself, and me, for not realizing that snow on the roof of the car made it blue and white, not blue and black, backing up the prediction I had made earlier.

A few weeks later, we were off to another party, and I again told Esther we were going to be in another snow-related pileup that night.

"Don't even kid like that," she said. "It's not funny. Besides, I watched the news earlier, and they didn't say anything about any snow tonight. So don't even start with me."

I wasn't kidding, I tried to warn her, but she didn't believe me.

We went into Brooklyn that night, and I did my readings. And, sure enough, when we got out it was snowing. We called a cab, and just like last time Esther insisted we exit the highway to drop her off. Again, I told her she was better off staying at my apartment and going home the next morning.

No sooner had the words come out of my mouth than we started to skid at almost the exact same place we had the other accident. I looked at Esther as we were spinning, and I saw her pull that hat down over here eyes, mumbling something unpleasant about my prediction.

To our surprise, we came to a stop without hitting anything. But then the cab stalled, and the driver couldn't get it started again. He told us not to worry, getting out of the car and popping open the hood to see if he could fix the problem.

After about ten minutes, Esther decided to get out, too, and asked me to join her. I declined. "I'll stay in the car," I told her, "and send energy to start it back up."

Little did she know, I wasn't going to do a thing. It was three in the morning, I was cold and tired, I wasn't about to freeze my butt off out there for no good reason. Besides, I'm psychic, not a mechanic. What did I know about fixing a car?

A few minutes passed, and Esther stuck her head back in the car to find out how my energy transfer was going, only to find me snoring away in the front seat. Angry, she placed her cold hands on my shoulders and shook me, demanding, "Where's the energy you promised? We're freezing out here trying to start the car and you're in here sleeping?"

"Who says I was sleeping?" I quickly shot back in my own defense. "You're talking a whole big engine here. I need to really concentrate in order to do that. It takes time. So go back out there. I'll call you when I'm ready."

To be honest, I still wasn't serious about restarting the car. I knew I couldn't do it. I was so tired, I didn't want to leave that warm car. So I made up the story about being able to channel my energy to the engine.

Eventually, Esther and the driver had had enough, and they flagged down a dilapidated van. We all piled in, but there were no seats in the back so every time the van made a turn we went flying, smashing into one another or the side doors. Esther was afraid one of us would go flying right out one of those doors.

When our ride from hell was over, I was never so happy to be back home. But I didn't hear the end of it for at least a month. The last thing Esther said that night was, "No more parties in Brooklyn. Ever. You hear me?"

Another funny incident was when Esther and I boarded an airplane headed to Florida. Esther hated to fly, but I had business there, and I needed her with me. All the way to the airport, and then getting on the plane, she kept asking me to make sure it was okay to take this flight. I would never make fun of Esther's fear, so I kept trying to get a reading about the flight for her every time she asked.

Everything was okay, as far as I could see, until we started to taxi down the runway. As the plane started to pick up speed for takeoff, I got a vision that someone on the plane had a gun. My face must have turned white because Esther asked me what was wrong. When I told her we needed to get off the plane, she screamed, ripping off her seat belt and jumping out of her seat, determined to get the captain's attention. One of the stewardesses saw her and came over to see what was going on. Esther had lost it completely by now, so the stewardess tried to soothe her while at the same time blocking her way to the cockpit.

With Esther arguing with the stewardess, I tried to decipher the information I was receiving. First, I turned to the man seated behind me and asked him what he did for a living. He told me that he was a toy gun salesman, and that he was on his way to a convention in Florida. I immediately told Esther to sit down, that everything was okay. Then I told the stewardess that Esther was fine, that she was just trying to help me because I had become a little nervous.

Once Esther settled down, I explained to her what had happened, but she didn't talk to me for the rest of the flight. She didn't say much when we got to Florida either, even though we shared a room. That is, until one night when I was having a problem sleeping. I kept the lights burning, and after a couple of hours of trying to fall asleep she jumped out of bed and yelled at me to shut them off.

I explained to Esther I couldn't sleep in the dark anywhere

there were ghosts. When I told her this, she went off the deep end. "How could you make me stay in a place where there were ghosts?" she demanded. Needless to say, she had trouble sleeping the rest of the trip.

Working with Josephine also was fun. She was an incredible worker, and I could never have made my career work without her. She was more than a secretary; she was my sidekick. And, more often than not, she was my driver.

Josephine always maintained a positive attitude; she was uplifting to be around. And she was like a sister to me. We both loved to interact with people and see how they lived, especially the wealthy. We both were chagrined that some of the wealthiest people were often some of the least generous, and the least friendly. When we would do readings, we were lucky to get a Coke. Forget the ice! On the other hand, it was the client who didn't have much who always treated us like royalty. He or she would lay out a spread fit for a king.

One time, Josephine chauffeured me to the home of a very rich family, and when we got there they served us Diet-Rite cola. As soon as Jo saw the cans, she knew it was going to be a long day. She knew how much I hated Diet-Rite, so she had a bad feeling about the whole thing.

Boy, was she ever right!

I don't remember what I had eaten that day before we got there, but I had the worst gas. I kept holding it in, holding it in, hoping it would go away. I just wanted to finish the reading without passing gas. If I did, no doubt I would lose her as a client.

Just when I thought I had made it, I let one rip walking to the door. Josephine was next to me, and I innocently inquired, "What was that?"

"Don't try to blame it on me," she answered without hesitation. "You farted!"

I was so embarrassed. I hadn't expected that Jo would lay the blame on me, out loud, right in front of the woman; I thought she'd let it pass, so to speak. I tried in vain to cover myself, but it only made things worse. "Sorry," I blurted out, "but that only happens when I drink cheap cola."

It is times like these you never forget. I was and am blessed to have people like Josephine and Esther in my life. I've learned about life the hard way. People go through hard times so they can come to know what really matters. You can't put a price on friendship and its importance in your life. People are what matter.

SEVEN

The Gift
of Sharing

*No medium can be one hundred percent
accurate. Fifty percent accuracy with a psychic
is desirable. Incredibly enough, Yolana has been
accurate to one hundred percent, and usually
operates in the eighty percent range. I
believe she's one of the great psychics of
this century.* —HANS HOLZER

Once the word got out that I could communicate with the dead, people from all walks of life came to me for readings, including the New York Police Department. While most police don't believe in what I do, I'm usually able to convince those who work with me. Most often, they want me to help them crack a murder case they can't solve using conventional methods. I show them how to find evidence where they never thought to look.

Sometimes, the police show me a piece of jewelry or clothing, or even a severed arm, and I am able to tell them who it belongs to, and who the killer is and where to find him. Sometimes, it's the spirit of the victim that speaks to me directly; other times, it's revealed in my mind's eye.

For instance, in March 1984 the police found two female

bodies in plastic bags dumped alongside a parkway in Harrison, New York. The girls, estimated to be between fifteen and nineteen years of age, had no identification on them, and any leads were minimal at best. All the police had to go on was the girls' clothing, some costume jewelry, and a pair of keys found on one of them.

Every conventional approach was tried to solve the case: autopsies were performed; letters with photographs were sent to all public and private schools in Westchester, the Bronx, and as far away as Fairfield, Connecticut; the National Crime Information Center, which compiles a list of missing persons around the country, was notified. And while NCIC came up with some seven hundred possibilities, nothing seemed to be a match.

Two detectives from Harrison, working for over a month on the case, were only able to discover that one of the keys found at the scene had been cut by a locksmith on Southern Boulevard, in the Bronx, so they shared this information with the local Bronx precinct. Now both precincts were looking to find the identities of the two young girls, so they could crack the mysterious double homicide. Posters with an artist's rendition of the girls were distributed all over the city, including the Bronx. Word of the mystery spread to the media, with reporters assigned to cover the case calling it the "Plastic Bag Murders."

Yet despite tireless efforts, doubling manpower, and the daily pressures from the media to solve the case, the police were still coming up empty. They were looking for help from anyone who could offer it. But when one reporter suggested bringing in a psychic, they all thought he was crazy.

That is, until one of the detectives gave in and called me. I'll never forget the reaction of the detective the first time I spoke with him on the phone regarding the case. Before he told me any of the details, I told him, "You have two girls in a wooded area in plastic bags."

Astonished, he still was incredulous, and asked me if I had read about the case in the newspapers. I told him I hadn't, and then told him about the blue van they had just found that might be linked to the murders.

That was enough for him. No one knew about that van except police assigned to this case. So this detective wanted to find out how I knew about this confidential information. Either someone was leaking it to me or I truly was psychic.

The detective wanted to meet with me right away, so I gave him my address, and told him to bring along photographs and whatever else he had so I could supply him with more details. Evidence allows me to get in tune with the crime scene, the victim, and the perpetrator. He showed up, tape recorder in hand, and I offered him some coffee, sensing he still wasn't convinced that I could help him, and wanting to put him at ease. As he sipped his coffee, I looked over what he had brought, including the medical examiner's photographs, and some very inexpensive, popular, and therefore basically untraceable jewelry that the girls had been wearing the night they were killed. Running my fingers over one of the photographs, I got my first bit of information. I told him I was seeing an anchor and a peacoat, like the ones sailors wear in the navy, around one of the girls. Prostitution was involved, I told him.

"No way," the detective cut me off almost immediately. "This girl had long underwear on, and I don't know any hookers who walk around like that."

Ignoring his comment, I went on with the reading, and the next thing that came up was the girl was bisexual. I also was getting the feeling that she might have been a topless dancer, because I was hearing loud music around her. Then I told him that she had been hit on the left side of her head just before she died.

"But the medical examiner found no trauma to her head," the doubting detective interrupted me again.

By then, I had had it. "I don't care what your medical examiner said. I'm telling you she was hit on the head before she died."

Picking up another photo, I told the detective that Connecticut was important to the case, as well as waterworks. Also, the girls were tied up *after* they died. In addition, the names Gomez, Perez, and Rivera kept popping up.

The detective was none too impressed with me. My information didn't jibe with what the police already had. The detective went so far as to say that the names I gave him were very common Hispanic ones, and checking them wasn't something they could do because it would take forever. But I knew differently. I insisted he take me to the crime scene so I could get more information.

Before driving there, the detective picked up his partner on the case. They told me we were going to check out the waterworks department, about two miles from where the bodies had been found. They didn't find anything there, making them more skeptical by the minute. But I tuned out their doubts and concentrated instead on the task at hand. I knew I was right.

When we started driving on the Hutchinson River Parkway toward the crime scene, I told the detectives that the killers hadn't driven this way. Once we arrived at the crime scene, which was near Harrison High School, I told them that something silver—something metallic—had been dropped there that night, something that would identify the people involved.

"Kids throw everything here," the detectives argued, "beer cans, soda cans, cigarettes, foil. So how do we know what silver thing to look for?"

I didn't have an answer. I could only tell them what had been revealed to me. What they didn't understand was that I don't control the information I relay. If I could tell them more, I would.

Then one of the detectives asked me about the girls' pocketbooks, and if I knew where they were. I pointed to a nearby drain, where they searched but found nothing. They then brought me home. So much for psychics! I knew they were thinking.

Finally, a few days later, there was a break in the case. A man and a woman had come to the police station to file a missing person's report on their daughter. As they were talking to an officer, one of the detectives on the Plastic Bag Murders couldn't help but overhear their description, and told them he might know where she was. He showed them photographs from the crime scene, then escorted them to the medical examiner's office to make a positive identification.

Sadly, it was their daughter. Her name was Iris Camacho. The Camachos hadn't reported her as missing sooner because she had a history of running away. She had gone missing once too often, and her parents thought she would turn up sooner or later, as usual.

Now detectives were hoping to identify the other girl, but no new leads were forthcoming. They talked to people who attended Iris's funeral; they talked with friends who had gone to school with her. No one knew who the other girl might be.

Talking with the Camachos, detectives found out that Iris loved to snap photographs, so they asked to take some of her pictures down to the station. Maybe Iris's photographs would help piece together who she had been murdered with and why they were killed.

Indeed, the pictures helped the detectives find out where Iris hung out and with whom. One photograph showed a group of young people standing in front of a club in the Bronx, so that's where the detectives headed. They located some of the people in the photograph, and they questioned them about Iris.

They learned Iris had been wild and uncontrollable, and deep into cocaine. They learned she liked older men—forty- to forty-five-year-olds—and that she would trade sex for drugs. The detectives recalled I had told them that prostitution might be involved. What made bells go off in their heads, however, was being told that Iris was sexually involved with a girl named Cookie. They remembered me telling them that one of the girls was bisexual.

The detectives began to admit that maybe there was something to what I was telling them, and they called me to tell me what they had found out and ask me if I had anything else for them about the case. I told them that the key they had found opened a red door. I also told them they were very close to cracking the case.

A week later, the second girl was identified when a woman called the precinct after seeing something about the unidentified girl in a local Hispanic newspaper. She thought the girl might be her friend's daughter Daisy. When the detectives got to the woman's home, they saw that her building was only four blocks from the locksmith where the key had been made. They also saw that the door to her apartment building was dark orange—close enough to red. When they tried the key in the door's lock, to their surprise it worked.

Pieces of the puzzle started falling into place. The woman who called the cops was Mrs. Gomez, and she told the detectives that Daisy's last name was Rivera. The detectives asked her about the third name I mentioned—Perez—and she said that was Daisy's stepfather's name. Mrs. Gomez then took them to Daisy's mother, who made a positive identification of the girl from the medical examiner's photographs, and from her jewelry. She, too, hadn't reported her daughter as missing because Daisy, like Iris, also would disappear from time to time. She also told the detectives that Daisy used to live in Bridgeport, Connecticut, and that she had recently enlisted in the navy, which tied into the peacoat image I got the first day the detective came to my apartment.

Daisy's mother allowed detectives to search Daisy's room. They left with a dresser drawer full of photographs and address books.

Again, the detectives called me with their findings, thoroughly impressed with the accuracy of my information. They teased me about being off about the color of the door, to which I responded, "Nobody's perfect, sweetheart!"

They asked if I would be willing to look at what they found in Daisy's dresser. I agreed, and the two detectives were at my door with a tape recorder in hand before you could say boo.

I examined the photographs, and one of them bothered me so much that I asked the detectives to turn off their tape recorder. It was of three men, and as soon as I rubbed the face of one of them with my finger I knew he was the killer. "This man is your killer," I told the detectives. The reason I requested that the recorder be shut off was fear that someday, somehow, the killer might hear the tape and come after me.

Jaws down to their knees, the detectives sat there amazed at what I had told them. They knew who the two other men in the photograph were, but they were clueless about the third. The two they knew were father and son, a man nicknamed Indio and his kid Pete, who owned a club on 161st Street and Union Avenue in the Bronx. I told them that Indio knew everything, and that Pete was the weak link. Because I also kept perceiving a Cuban connection with the third man, I asked the detectives if Cuba had anything to do with the case. They had no idea.

The detectives went right away to interview Indio and Pete to get some answers. They caught the two in a number of lies, but they did find out that the other man in the photo was nicknamed Cuba, and that he was a drug dealer in the neighborhood. Indio and Pete also gave them Cuba's address, and the detectives headed over to his building, a tenement, on Dekalb Avenue, right across the street from North Central Bronx Hospital.

Cuba was the building's super and lived in the basement. The detectives later said they had had a bad feeling about him from the minute they met him. Even though he gave them no new information, they sensed he was involved just by his reaction—or lack of reaction—to their questioning: he had no expression on his face when they talked to him. Too, his apartment was a mess, and there were raunchy posters of naked women plastering the walls. The whole thing gave them the creeps.

Even though the detectives felt that they had their suspects, they didn't have a case because there was no evidence placing the men at the scene of the crime. They then took me to Indio's bar to see if I could pick up on anything. As soon as we got within blocks of the place, I started receiving information about the case, information that initially was of no help to the detectives because I was speaking Spanish, a language they nor I knew a word of. Now that I think back on it, Daisy must have been coming to them through me, and telling them what they wanted to know. All I could remember coming out of the trance was the name Cuba and, oddly enough, the smell of soot.

With no other leads, the detectives felt they needed to pressure one of the men into talking. A plan was hatched to get Pete and Indio to confess. They would involve Pete in a three-way drug deal with two undercover police officers at the club. The first buy, for between three and four thousand dollars, went over without a hitch. The second, for ten thousand, arranged for a few weeks later at a local diner, was overpriced on purpose so that Pete would be sure to show up. The only problem was, the precinct could come up with only four thousand in cash, so one of the detectives went to his bank to take out a second mortgage on his house. That's how much he wanted to snare the murderers, and how much he trusted my information that these men did it. Fortunately, the bank gave him the money outright, and once they found out what it was for agreed that it would be considered a formal loan only if he lost the money and couldn't pay it back in a few days.

The drug deal went down on a Friday night. The detectives were backed up by at least fifteen police officers inside the diner posing as chefs, waiters, busboys, and customers, making sure that the dealer didn't get away and make off with the money. It apparently looked like something right out of a movie.

The buy went just like clockwork, with Pete and his friends expecting to score but instead they walked away empty-handed— empty-handed but in handcuffs. Seven people were arrested that night, including Pete. Everyone except him was booked in the Bronx. He was transported to Harrison, where police interrogated him about the Plastic Bag Murders.

It only took a few minutes for Pete to confess once a photograph of Daisy was shoved in his face. Just like I predicted, he was the weak link, and he told them everything they needed to know. They videotaped his statement, in which he confessed, detail by detail, what had happened that night.

Pete said that he had gone to the club Sunday night (February 5) around ten, and one of his employees told him that his father had gone with Iris to Cuba's house earlier, around seven. When Pete arrived at Cuba's, a man named Vaquero answered the door armed with a machine gun. Inside, Pete saw his father sitting on a couch with Iris. Cuba and a man named Nino stood nearby, guns in hand.

Daisy, tied up and seated in a chair, was wrapped up to her waist in a plastic bag. She wasn't hurt, however. An argument was going on, with Cuba accusing Indio, Iris, and Daisy of plotting to steal his drugs and Indio defending the three.

The argument went on for half an hour to forty-five minutes, and at one point Cuba announced that he was gonna kill everybody. He then began calling Iris names, tied her up and put her in a plastic bag, too. Snorting coke, Cuba started torturing both Iris and Daisy, and tormenting Indio and Pete with what he was going to do to them. Around eleven-thirty, Vacquero asked Cuba what they were going to do, and at that Cuba gagged Daisy, put a bag over her head, tied a rope around her neck, and choked her to death. He then slipped a third bag over her entire body, then, tying her hands to her feet, contorted her into a fetal position.

Iris, also gagged by now, began to panic and struggle after witnessing Daisy's fate. Cuba hit her on the side of the head—just as I had foreseen weeks earlier—knocking her unconscious. With Iris now down, Cuba wrapped cord around her neck and choked the life out of her. He celebrated by doing more coke, even sharing it, and passed around a bottle of whiskey while discussing what to do with the bodies.

"You two dump them," Cuba told Indio and Pete. "Don't worry—if we're stopped by the cops, we'll kill them, too."

Before they left, Cuba had them remove the bags, untie and untape the girls, and retie and rebag them more efficiently to make it easier to put them in the van. This step confirmed another prediction of mine: that the victims were tied up postmortem.

Initially, they planned to dump the bodies on City Island, but first icy roads and then a friendly offer to help from a bus driver who saw them skid off the side of the road made for a change of plans. They decided to dump the bodies upstate, so they took Route 95 to Harrison—again echoing my theory that the killers did not use the Hutchinson River Parkway—and unloaded the bodies near Union Avenue when their car again started to skid on the ice. When asked to describe this in more detail, Pete mentioned that his silver key chain had broken when they were dumping the bodies, which caused the detective to do a double take: I had told him to look for something silver when examining the crime scene.

After Pete told the detectives all he knew, Indio also came clean and turned state's witness. Police now wanted Cuba's head on a platter, so they gathered a force of some twenty-five personnel: ten from the Westchester DA's office, eight from the Westchester police department, five from the Harrison police department, and the two detectives from the Bronx who had been on the case from the beginning. Vehicles, firepower, and bullet-proof vests backed up the manpower. They were taking this guy down.

They stormed Cuba's basement apartment, hoping to drag him out alive. On the way in, one of the detectives smelled soot, and remembered the connection I'd made earlier. It was coming from the boiler room, which was directly across from Cuba's place.

The plan was to knock on Cuba's door and rush in as soon as he opened it. But the door was already open, and Cuba wasn't there. Some naked guy was asleep on the bed, and when the detectives woke the startled man up he told them that he didn't know where Cuba was. Outside, however, construction workers told them that Cuba was down the street in a diner on Dekalb Avenue eating breakfast.

On the way, one of the detectives saw Cuba talking on a pay phone, and, without hesitation, he approached him from behind and put a gun to his head. He was being placed under arrest for the murders of Daisy and Iris, the detective informed Cuba.

Eventually, Antonio Delasmatas-Bujosa, aka Cuba, José Ramos, aka Nino, and Ramon Vaquero were convicted of second-degree murder and sentenced to prison.

Eight months later, a big blue-and-white sign was erected on the scene of the crime. WESTCHESTER WATERWORKS WILL BE WORKING IN THIS AREA, it announced, fulfilling yet another prediction.

I am not telling this story to show you how accurate my readings are or how good I am at what I do. I want you to understand that I don't say things just to say them. I share information in order to help people. Whether it's detectives trying to solve a murder case, or someone trying to find out if a spouse is cheating, it doesn't matter to me. I don't censor, and I don't make up things. I'll tell what I see and that's it.

My psychic gift is too precious to me to tamper with or take lightly. We all suffer pain, so if I can alleviate some of that pain through what I perceive psychically I will. God gave me this gift, and I want to share it.

EIGHT

Let Your Spirit Be Your Guide

Some people may wonder, where does Yolana get the information she gives to her clients when she does readings? Does she get it from her own extrasensory perception, or does she tap some deep source where everything is listed? Or are there spirit guides who whisper into her ear and she repeats what she hears?

All three are possible, and I'm very open-minded about this. Most conventional parapsychologists are bothered by the idea of guides and an afterlife. They are incapable of accepting the idea, but I don't agree. —HANS HOLZER

I think all of us are born with psychic powers, but people like myself—so-called psychics—have a better ability to tap into the spirit world than others. As a matter of fact, I believe that each of us has our very own spirit guides to direct us.

To be in tune with your psychic self, the first thing you need to do is be in tune with your spirit guide, to let your spirit be your guide. Forget letting your conscience be your guide. Each of us is assigned a guide (or guides) at birth. The more we listen to those guides, the better off we'll be.

My spirit guide's name is Max. He's been with me since I was very young. I can remember playing with him when I was four or five years old. And I had long conversations with him, thinking nothing strange about it. I thought everyone had an imaginary friend. Come to think of it, I was right.

Max appears to me when I least expect it. He is a good-looking thirty- to forty-year-old, with black hair and brown eyes. Sometimes he's dressed in an old-fashioned way; other times, he's quite up to date.

The first time I saw Max, my parents were putting me to bed, and as soon as they left the room he appeared. He had a centaur with him, a half horse/half man, a creature right out of Greek mythology. Why the centaur was with him, I don't know. Maybe Max knew I loved horses, and figured I would be less frightened if he had a horselike animal with him. Maybe it was his way of luring me into his world.

The next morning, I told my mother about the visit, pointing out the hoofprints in the rug around my bed. She didn't seem the least bit shocked, so I concluded such visits were normal. And from an early age, I had been taught that everybody has a guardian angel so I just assumed that Max was mine.

From the very start, Max has always made me feel at ease. Always playful, he nonetheless is there to cheer me up or help me if I am sad or need him.

For instance, when Marvin would have one of his episodes and come after me, Max would always intervene and either slow Marvin down or push him aside completely so I could get away. Max also is with me whenever I go into a trance, making sure I come out of it unharmed.

Hans Holzer taught me that going into a trance is not something to be taken lightly because you open up your "psychic door" and you have no way of knowing what will pass through that door. Although not dealing with demons or the devil, one may be dealing with a spirit who has some serious unfinished business to attend to. Max is there to keep an eye on me in such situations.

But when Max is not being serious, he likes to have fun. He has a great sense of humor like me, so it's no wonder he was chosen to be my guide. Over the years, we've had many laughs together, and that's been a real godsend for me, especially during the difficult times in my life. On countless occasions, Max almost got me thrown out of the Martha Washington Hotel. He and I would be talking about something, laughing hard, and the other residents would complain I was breaking the rules, bringing men up to my room. Little did they know that my man was a spirit.

Max has been there to guide and protect me, especially when times got tough. He would prepare me to face the bad things, to keep on the right path when I seemed to get lost. Now, you may be asking yourself, If Max was such a good guide, why did he allow Yolana to go through so much suffering before he allowed her to turn her life around?

You have to understand, I had to go through the bad in order to grow spiritually. We all have trials in life in order to learn valuable lessons, and I'm no exception. Just because I'm in contact with the Other Side doesn't mean I have a free pass through life. I had to learn my own life lessons, and no one—not even a spirit guide— can do that for you.

Trust me, though, your guide is with you all the time, even when you feel all alone. Guides direct and protect us, especially when the going gets rough. They may not give us all the answers, but they are by our side.

Max, in fact, is my main connection to the Other Side. He is the coin that activates the telephone that allows me to communicate with people who have passed over into the other dimension. But just because I'm psychic doesn't mean my guide gives me more direction and answers than your guide does. All of us have the power to get in touch with the spirits who guide us. Perhaps you haven't met your spirit guide yet, or maybe your psychic door hasn't been opened all the way. Or maybe you are in denial about what you have seen or heard over the years. Maybe you have dismissed these experiences as coincidence, or figments of the imagination. There is no such thing as coincidence—it doesn't exist. If you met your future mate in one place when you were supposed to be somewhere else, that's not coincidence. Both of your spirit guides were at work. Spirits don't make us make decisions; they just try to guide us when making them.

So pay attention to the voice in your head. The sooner you listen, the sooner you will come to know your guide.

Just because I'm in tune with my guide Max doesn't make me better than you. It just means I'm more aware of and open to the Other Side than you at this time. People are afraid of what's on the Other Side, so they try to ignore anything to do with it. They pretend not to perceive what their guides have presented to them. But trust me, your guide is keeping an eye out on you.

If you haven't seen any signs, pay closer attention: you're getting them all the time because your guide is giving them to you all the time, leading you in the right direction. Your guide could be anybody from a past life. We knew our guides in a previous lifetime, and we choose whether or not to be with them in this lifetime.

It makes no difference whether you're given a man or a woman for a guide: there is no gender in the spirit world. My guide probably appears to me as a man because I've always needed a strong presence in my life because of the rough life I have led and, to me, men are symbols of strength, so I guess that's why I got Max. And I wouldn't have it any other way. He's always been there for me, and I'm convinced he always will be until the day I die.

> *Max is my mother's security.*
> *He watches out for her and protects her.*
> —MELODY BARD RANDAZZO

As far as there being any other spirit guides in my life, I think Max is it. But I could be wrong. Max is the only one I'm aware of. I'm also so in tune with Max, maybe that doesn't allow other spirits to come through. So while it could be somebody else telling me something, I'm thinking it's got to be Max. When I "hear" a psychic message, I assume it's Max. Over the years, I've also learned that Max likes to be the center of attention. So even if someone else has a message for me, Max wants to be the one to give it to me.

Max liked to show himself every so often to the people who worked for me, such as Josephine. I remember one night she and I were going out for a steak dinner after a hectic day of readings at my apartment. We decided on the famous Manhattan steakhouse Smith & Wollensky. We rushed out of the apartment and hailed the first cab we saw, both so hungry that we couldn't wait to sit down to a nice meal. But when we were finally seated at the restaurant, Josephine realized that she didn't have her pocketbook with her. She couldn't remember if she had left it in the cab or at the apartment, so we had to go back to the apartment to see if it was there.

Back at the apartment, Jo didn't find her pocketbook on the couch where she usually left it, so she started to get really nervous. As she became more agitated, trying to figure out what to do next, Max is laughing, having a hell of a time watching her lose it.

Now, I knew what had happened to her bag. So I went to my closet, and, lo and behold, there was Josephine's bag, at the bottom of my closet, under all my shoes.

Max loves hiding people's things, especially keys, when they come to my apartment, and he especially loved to fool around with Josephine because both are clowns. But Jo wasn't laughing that night. When she didn't see her pocketbook on the couch, she thought she'd lost everything—wallet, money, keys. So when I found her bag, she was relieved but also angry. She vowed to never let her bag out of her sight again whenever she came to my apartment, and swore that this would be the last time Max would pull a stunt like that on her.

But Jo met her match in Max, and he didn't wait long to stage another prank. After finding the bag, we headed back to Smith & Wollensky. Now we were so hungry we could have eaten a horse. When the bill came, Jo generously offered to cover it. But then when she reached for her wallet, she noticed her keys were missing. She frantically searched through her bag but couldn't find them. I told her to look under the dessert menu, but she ignored me. You see, her big key chain not only had what seemed like all the keys to the city on it but also a big name tag, so how could it possibly be under the menu? Yet when the waiter took the menus away, her keys fell out of hers onto the table.

Another time, Jo and I were heading to a reading, and just as she was about to slip into the driver's seat she spun around like a top and landed facedown in my lap in the front seat. Confused, she asked me what she had tripped on. I told her it was just Max: he wanted to get in first.

But dealing with spirits isn't always fun and games. While your guide always has your best interests in mind, that is not necessarily the case with other spirits. Some of them can be quite mischievous, others can be downright evil. That's why I tell people never to play with a Ouija board. When you fool around with a Ouija board you are calling up spirits, and you don't know who or what you may be summoning. You have no idea which spirit or spirits will answer you.

Remember when I looked in the mirror and saw the devil? I must have summoned up some kind of evil spirit then, and, at the time, I had no idea what I was doing. It's no joke when you call up the spirit world. That's why I thank my lucky stars that I am blessed with a guide like Max and a mentor like Hans Holzer.

There is neither a devil, nor is there demonic possession, in my opinion, but there are cases on record of evil or disturbed people who have passed on and have taken hold of the mind of a certain individual in order to be able to continue their existence.

Possession is not a fantasy; it is a fact!

—HANS HOLZER

I recall the case of a possessed woman who lived in Philadelphia. Her husband contacted Hans and made arrangements for them to come up to New York to see him. Hans then contacted me, telling me what he wanted to do for this couple. He wanted me to help him coax the evil spirit out of the woman's body. The idea is to convince the entity to exit the victim and enter the medium and then exit the scene altogether. It's a dangerous process, however, again because you don't know who or what you're dealing with.

Hans learned from the husband that they recently had moved into a house in which hauntings had been documented, and that the wife took medication. The reason this second piece of information was important is that drugs make it easier for a spirit to open the psychic door. Possession is possible only when the possessed is weak due to drugs, alcohol, or a specific mental condition.

A few days after the husband firmed up plans with Hans, he called back in a frantic state. His wife had gone off the deep end, and he asked if he could bring her to New York immediately.

The husband, a wealthy businessman, had consulted some well-respected Philadelphia doctors about her case, and they all recommended that she be institutionalized for what they diagnosed as a schizophrenic disorder. While Hans desperately wanted to help the man, he was scheduled to go to California on important business and he couldn't cancel, but he offered to treat her there if the couple was willing to fly out and meet him. Without hesitating, the man agreed, and also paid for my ticket to California as well.

The four of us eventually met up at the Westwood Marquis in Los Angeles. There, we attempted to extract the possessor from the woman's body.

The first step in coaxing an entity out is to make it show itself or make itself heard. Through suggestion, Hans put me into a receptive state resembling hypnosis, and I became very relaxed both physically and mentally. Then he asked the spirit to use me as a spokesperson. And the spirit did just that.

In that state, I had no idea what was going on. The spirit apparently spoke through me, using not only his own voice but his own facial expressions, his own personality, even his own hair color. Meanwhile, Hans put the woman under hypnosis, and suggested that she keep her psychic door closed. Then he turned his attention back to me, and to the possessor coming through me. He employed what is known as the "rescue circle technique," meaning that one makes the possessing entity aware of who it is and that it is really dead. You see, spirits possessing people think they are still alive and need bodies to inhabit. Once they become aware that they are dead, they rest easy, and cross over from this earthly plane to the Other Side. There's no point in the spirit possessing another person if the spirit isn't alive.

You want to rescue both the entity and the person possessed. You don't want a psychic or a clairvoyant for this kind of work. You need a trance medium in order for the spirit to speak through him or her. In addition, a trained parapsychologist must be present because when you open the psychic door of the trance medium, you have no way of knowing what will pass in or out.

In order to deal with the entity—to assure that it will do your bidding—you must have an undiluted sense of authority; there can be absolutely no question about who is in charge. I sent one man packing by telling him, in no uncertain terms, who he was, that he was dead, and that he had to go to where he belonged. It was clear he had heard me because Yolana soon quieted down and we felt no presence at all.

The cases of true possession are very few and far between. The medical profession usually misses such cases because they either don't know or don't recognize the symptoms, and often people are institutionalized as a schizophrenic when, in fact, they are possessed.

Trance is a great responsibility, and it often can involve physical as well as mental danger if the trance medium is unattended, so I asked Yolana not to go into trance except in my presence or when specific police work requires it. —HANS HOLZER

Although dealing with possession is dangerous, I trust Hans Holzer completely. He knows what he is doing, and I know he always looks out for my well-being. To my way of thinking, there is nobody better in the field than him. I thank my lucky stars every day that I was blessed with a spirit guide like Max and an earthside guide like Holzer. Without Hans and Max, I'd be lost. Over the years, I've learned that we get guidance from many different sources. Max, my spirit guide, has walked with me through life every step of the way. Hans has been there to help me understand those steps.

NINE

I See Dead
and
Live People

While being a psychic requires that I communicate with the dead from time to time, on a day-to-day basis the job requires communicating with the living—my clients. Essentially, I help them get to the right spot when they come for a reading with me.

Let's say a client's main question is about her relationship, which has all sorts of problems. Deep down, she may know there's no chance of saving it, but she wants to know what I see in store for her and her partner in the future.

If there is a way I can help save a client's relationship, believe me, I will. If not, I feel it's my job to help the client get to a point where the breakup will be less painful. I may suggest psychological counseling if I see that the breakup is going to be traumatic.

Often, clients come to me blaming themselves for the problems in the relationship, believing that they alone are responsible for it not working. Yet nine out of ten times, they couldn't be further from the truth. It may be the partner's fault. Or, believe it or not, the fault of neither.

For instance, I may pick up that the partner had a very hard upbringing with emotional, and perhaps physical, abuse. By showing the client that the problems are rooted in the partner's past, that neither of them is responsible, it allows them to work on the root cause instead of playing the blame game.

When reading people with relationship problems, I try to ascertain if the client and partner are good friends. For me, a healthy relationship means being good friends first, lovers second. Be a good friend, and you and your partner can overcome almost anything. But if sexual love is all you have in the relationship, it's not enough. Friendship makes a relationship work. If the client can look me in the eye and tell me that, honestly, she is best friends with her partner, then I tell her the relationship is worth saving.

But to get honest answers from my clients about such personal matters, I need for them to feel comfortable with me from the minute they walk through my door, especially if they're coming to see me for the first time. They need to relax and be clear-headed, so they understand the information I'm receiving during the reading and absorb what I'm telling them about it. If they are not relaxed and comfortable, chances are they will get what mediums call "psychic amnesia," where they forget things they otherwise know like the back of their hand.

Recall what happened to Josephine the first time I read her: she couldn't even remember the name of her husband—the man she woke up next to every morning. People can go blank for a moment. It happens a lot during someone's first reading. I've had clients tell me that riding down in the elevator after a reading, they suddenly realize who or what I had been talking about.

Therefore, for a first reading I have a set routine. Either my daughter Melody or my assistant Ben Autieri greets the client at the door and welcomes him or her to my home. The client is invited to sit down in the living room, and offered coffee, tea, or a soft drink while waiting for me to emerge from the bedroom, where I do all my readings.

First, I sit with the client in the living room for a little while. If I just have finished a reading, it allows me to relax and recharge. And it also allows my psychic eye to focus on the new client. I'll sip some coffee and make small talk so we can connect before going into the other room and getting down to business. This breaking of the ice may take anywhere from a minute or two up to ten or fifteen minutes, before I ask, "Are you ready?" and I lead the client to the reading.

As soon as we are in the bedroom, I focus only on the reading. To avoid distraction, I keep my bedroom as neutral yet as comfortable as possible. No pictures on the wall, no clutter. I need the client's undivided attention.

Clients are asked to bring photographs of people who are close to them or who they want to know about in this reading. They also are given the option of bringing along a cassette tape in case they want me to record the reading.

The reason I have people bring photographs is because I feel a piece of a person's life goes into every picture that's taken. You know how in the old movies the Indian would always refuse to let his picture be taken because he felt that people were trying to steal his soul? Well, it's something like that, except that photos aren't *that* powerful, but they do let me get a person's energy as I touch it.

I suggest the client bring a cassette tape to record the session so that he or she can review the readings later. I find that many people are especially nervous at their first reading and miss a lot of the information.

Most clients, in fact, usually are nervous, so once we are seated at the table with the photographs between us I let them know exactly what to expect.

I tell them that I pick up names from the past, present, and future, explaining further that if they don't recognize names during the reading itself they will in the future, and that they can call me then and we can talk. They will understand then why I mentioned the name during the reading.

I also like to let clients know how I receive information. When I "see" or "hear" something during a reading, I explain, I don't actually see with my eyes or hear with my ears. I get information through my "psychic eye."

What's *that* like? clients constantly want to know.

Try describing the color orange to someone who is blind, I tell them. Pretty difficult, isn't it? That's what describing what I perceive is like. It's intuitive.

Next, I run my fingertips over the photographs. My fingertips are like antennae that allow me to pick up people's energy. Try it. Press your hands together and feel the energy between them. That's similar to the feeling I get when I touch photographs.

Touching the pictures starts my psychic wheels turning. I don't look at the photo all that closely; I usually close my eyes and just feel the energy. That lets me get into the physical being of the photographed individual. I can tell if the person has a sore leg, glaucoma, even something as major as cancer. I can gather this information without photographs, but it's easier with them.

The best photographs for me depict one person only; group shots give off too much, potentially confusing, information. It's like there's too much "noise" interfering with the person I'm trying to "hear."

Although I allow recording of the reading, sometimes I might turn the machine off if the information is of a confidential nature. I want to protect the person I'm talking about. I also want to safeguard the client and myself.

Once I told a client her husband needed psychiatric care, and when he heard the tape when she got home, he wanted to punch my lights out. Just what I *don't* need.

Having rubbed my fingertips over the photographs, I'll begin asking questions. Who's John? Who's Jane? Do they mean anything to you?

The names are specific to the client—some quite foreign— and the client validates them for me as soon as she recognizes them. It's not always easy pronouncing names correctly, but it's vital my clients know who I'm talking about. Then I describe everything I'm getting about these people, how they may affect the client's life.

Some people hear what I have to tell them and they respond, "No, that just can't be." They tell me I'm wrong.

I assure them I'm not making it up. Some things I say may sound like they are coming out of left field, but when information comes to me I get the strong scent of roses or feel a tug on my cheek or my head turns as if it's being pulled. So if I say, "You're pregnant," and the client protests, "No way," and I'm smelling roses, there's no chance I'm wrong.

Besides getting information about the future, I also get messages for clients that pertain to the present: what's going on with their relationships, their career, their home, their car, or even where their lost dog is.

I once did a reading for a cocky eighteen-year-old from Brooklyn. He came to me, he said, because he had nothing better to do that night. His best friend Gary's mom, Rose, used to throw psychic parties at her house in the 1980s, and she would always call me up to give her friends readings. I made good money doing six to eight readings at a pop. She and her son were always recommending me to new clients. Anyway, Gary would tell this friend to get a reading from me every time his mom had one of these parties, but this kid didn't want any part of it. He would tell Gary that he had no interest in having his "fortune told," and that he really didn't believe in psychics or swamis and their so-called powers to communicate with the Other Side. Until one rainy Friday night when he was at Gary's and I was there giving readings. Their dates had fallen through—they had been stood up—so they were watching the Rangers–Islanders game on cable instead.

As fate would have it—I don't believe in coincidences—one of Rose's friends called at the last minute and canceled. With her time slot for a reading now open, Rose asked Gary if he wanted it. He declined but nominated his friend instead. Embarrassed, and not wanting to say no to his best friend's mom, the friend agreed despite earlier resistance. Since he lived across the street, he went right home to collect some photographs for the reading.

When he returned, he explained to Gary and his friend's mother that he was willing to go along with the reading not because he believed in psychics but because he would "try anything once." He let them know he wasn't planning to say a word in the reading, that he "was going to sit there with my hands folded and see what she tells me." He didn't want to provide any information to help me with the reading because he thought that was how fortune-tellers and palm readers made clients believe what they told them.

But that wasn't his only plan. He showed one of the photographs to Gary. It was a picture of his cousin's white dog, which resembled Petey of *Little Rascals* fame, and which had run away a few weeks previous. He wanted to see just what I would get from the picture. He wasn't coming to me so I could help him; he was shelling out thirty dollars that night to test me, to prove me wrong, and to shut his friend up once and for all about all this psychic stuff.

Little did he know that skepticism doesn't intimidate me. I'm being tested every time I sit down to do a reading, whether it's the person's first time or the twenty-first. No matter who it is, I'm only as good as my last reading. But only about one percent of people who come to see me are what I call "testers." These testers want to see if I can really connect with the spirit world. But even these skeptics wind up coming back, once they test me. I always manage to tell them one little thing in the reading that only they knew about, and they become believers. So, in the end, I enjoy skeptics because I enjoy proving them wrong.

And for those skeptics who refuse to be won over no matter what, it's their problem. The information I'm getting is valid, and it's meant for them. If they're not interested in listening, it's their loss.

Anyway, Gary's friend handed me the pictures when we sat down for his reading, and crossed his arms across his chest, as if to say, Show me what you got, lady. I immediately started naming names—his mother, her father, his two brothers—right off the bat. I told him about the woman he would marry—what she looks like, that they would get married in their thirties, that they both would be working in a creative field, possibly as writers.

He wasn't impressed.

Then I told him that the car he and his brother were sharing needed fixing.

He still was not impressed, even though later I found he knew about the problem but wouldn't admit it. He wore his game face the whole time, like he promised Gary he would.

After giving him some more information about his life and future and him still not responding, I finally got him to talk when I told him NBC would be calling in two weeks, offering him a job in their sports division.

"Lady," he shot back, "I don't know what you're talking about. First of all, I already have a job [driving an ice-cream truck]. Second, I don't even know anyone at NBC. So how can you make a statement like that?"

I went on to tell him that I was getting a strong pull around him concerning the writing and communications fields—especially in the arena of professional sports.

He admitted to loving sports, and having an interest in writing, but he said that he was still undecided about what he wanted to major in when he went to college the next year. In fact, he didn't even know where he was going to college, whether he would go out of state or accept an offer from a local university.

Don't bother packing your bags, I told him, because you're staying in New York—Queens, as a matter of fact.

He looked at me even more skeptically, saying he despised Queens, and would never think of going to college there.

My guides kept spitting out NBC at me. They also told me he would work in front and behind the cameras in both the television and movie industries, and someday write books. When I told him this, he looked like he had had enough. But I wasn't done yet. I still had one more photograph left: the one of the dog.

I took it in my hand and immediately fell in love with the dog. I told Gary's friend how precious I thought that dog was, but he wasn't listening—he was tuning me out. Then something I said caught his attention. "Patches will be all right," I said. "Tell your cousins he's okay. He's living with a new family not far from their house, and they can go get him back if they like. He's in a yard with a lot of kids. As a matter of fact, he's living near a park that's surrounded by water on a street named . . ." And so on.

Well, nailing the dog's name won this client over. Patches was not a common name for a dog. But what really won him over didn't happen until three weeks later.

He had just about forgotten about my prediction that he'd be getting a call from NBC about a job opening, mostly because I said it would happen two weeks after the reading and the two weeks had come and gone.

But a week later, he was running late for a softball game, and he made a quick stop at his house to pick up his glove and jersey. On his way out, the phone rang, and his mother picked it up. It was his dad. His mom said the boy was running late for his game, that he couldn't talk. But his father insisted, so she handed her son the phone.

His father told him that he had one of his good friends sitting in his office, and that the friend wanted to say hello.

The friend introduced himself, saying he was the head sports cameraman at NBC. He then offered the boy a summer internship.

The boy had no idea his father knew anyone at NBC, let alone a bigwig in the sports department. He went in for an interview and met with Marv Albert and Len Berman—the station sports anchors at the time—and Sue Simmons and Tom Brokaw. And even though he didn't get the internship—he needed to be enrolled in college to be eligible—he did stay in the local area, enrolling at St. John's University in Jamaica, Queens.

Four years later, Gary's friend graduated, with a B.S. in journalism, and went on to become a sportswriter and a *New York Times* best-selling author. He married in his thirties. His wife, Denise, is an editor at Penguin, and she just so happens to be the editor of this book.

Now, how's that for turning a skeptic around?

TEN

Just
One More
Question

*P*eople come to me for two reasons. Some want to verify that a loved one who has died is all right and still connected to them. Others want something, and they want me to tell them if and when they will get it.

Over the years, I've found out that people will move mountains to find out if deceased relatives are okay. But they are even more obsessive about love. Clients want to know when they will find their "soul mate," or if the person they're already with is "the one."

These clients are the most difficult to read because they have no sense of reality. The world revolves around their relationship, and they hear only what they want to hear. I'm fighting an uphill battle with them if I say something that they don't like. No matter what, they won't believe it. And when I say something is going to take longer than they want it to, they dismiss it completely. When things don't work out the way they want them to, they look at me as if to say, What good are you?

When it comes to love and relationships, some clients are at their worst. They feel they are not whole people unless they have someone to love them. I tell them that the real key to happiness is to love and respect yourself, and that everything else will fall into place.

It's a message that usually doesn't get through, however. People are convinced that life is not worth living unless they have that one particular person.

When people ask my daughter Melody, who also has psychic abilities, why she doesn't become a professional psychic like her mother, she always says she simply doesn't have the patience to deal with people the way I do. She says I'm more of the diplomat, and that if she had to deal with people so blinded by what they think love is she would lose it and yell at them to get a grip.

I can't do that. Clients come to me for help, and I help them be the person they were meant to be and enjoy life. But it's not that easy.

One client has been in love with the same man for twelve years. I dread hearing from her, she's so obsessed. She goes to any lengths to try to corral this man she wants so badly but can't have. No matter what I tell her, she won't listen.

People often have a great life but just don't see it. It's not what they want. They aren't happy with who they are with or what they have or where they live. They always want more. But they don't realize that even if they get that stuff, they wouldn't be happy.

It's like the tale "The Fisherman and His Wife," where a poor fisherman spares the life of a talking flounder he catches one day. The flounder claims he's really a prince under a spell, and that it would be in the fisherman's best interest to let him go. The fisherman lets the flounder go, asking nothing in return.

When the fisherman returns to his broken-down shack empty-handed, and he tells his wife what happened, she tells him to go back and demand that the flounder/prince grant him a better home.

The flounder/prince grants the fisherman's wife's wish, and many more as she keeps sending him back. She even wants to be emperor, then pope.

Instead of being satisfied, the wife sends her husband back one last time, telling him to ask the flounder/prince to make her lord of the universe—in other words, to make her God.

This wish the fish won't grant. In fact, he takes back all the previously granted wishes. Clearly, she'd never be satisfied.

I feel like that flounder sometimes. Here I am, trying to please everybody, but some people you just can't please. And some people place too much emphasis on material things. Material possessions won't make you happy, I often admonish clients.

Now, don't get me wrong. I sometimes get caught up in this way of thinking. I'm human, just like you. I see people on television with big houses and fancy cars, and I witness up close how some of my wealthy clients live, and sometimes I wish I had that stuff, too. But I don't.

People assume my life's like the celebrities I read for, and when they come to my modest home for a reading they think I must have a second, more luxurious apartment somewhere else.

One client even thought I had a heliport on the roof of the building where a helicopter would whoosh me away to my real home once I finished my readings.

The truth is, I lead a very ordinary life. Sure, it's much better than when I was on the street, but I'm certainly no Donald Trump.

Too, people think that, being so in tune with the spirit world, I must lead this ultra-spiritual life. Wrong. I have the same emotions, and fight the same demons, that everyone else does.

Like the time my television blew out. I thought it was the end of the world. I couldn't imagine what I was going to do without it. I was really upset. But then I remembered what I tell my clients and I had to give myself a wake-up call. Listen, I said to myself, you lived in the gutter, and now you're attached to a television. What's up with that?

People just don't understand. They seem to value material possessions above all else. As if *things* are the most important key to happiness, as if having that big house or certain car or expensive jewels will bring instant and lasting fulfillment. But this is so untrue. Look at all the rich and famous people who have everything we long for and yet they are still unhappy. They want more and more. Millions aren't enough. They want billions. And then even more doesn't bring satisfaction. People mistakenly think that becoming rich and famous will make you happy, but life doesn't work that way. The only thing that will truly make us happy is fulfilling the purpose we are here to fulfill—learning the lessons we are supposed to learn. Until we learn those lessons, we'll be going round and round trying to find satisfaction but only coming up empty. People seem to expect things out of life, as if they're entitled to riches and fine things. But the best we can expect is to be at peace with ourselves. And that only happens when we learn the lessons we need to learn and accept ourselves for who we are.

Material things don't matter. Material things are transient—they don't last, they can be taken away at any moment.

I have always maintained that almost everybody is just one paycheck away from being on the street. Think about it.

One bad break and you're in the gutter. Or you're all alone. Or both. In reality, none of us is any better than people living on the street.

Name one material thing you truly own and I say it can be gone just like that. There is nothing that can't be taken from your grasp except your soul. That's all you truly own.

Think about how people are always worrying about material things. No one ever seems to worry what's going to happen to his or her soul. "Wish in one hand and crap in the other," my mother used to say. "Which hand do you think will have more in it when you are done?"

I have clients with absolutely heartbreaking stories. They have lost friends, spouses, even children. It just about kills me to hear some of these stories, and I would do anything to help them.

Then there are other clients who want nothing more than for me to reunite them with their lover—the same lover who cheated on them time and again—or to supply them with a winning lottery number. Them, I want to shake.

Hard as it is for some people to believe, being a psychic is not easy. Everyone wants to be able to do what I do. People think being psychic makes life better. After all, wouldn't you have all the answers—and riches—the world has to offer?

I'm here to tell you that such is not the case. I can't read my own future, for instance. And I have a hard time reading my children's. They are too close to me.

When I do a reading, I can't have a preconceived idea about the client; I can't have any emotional attachment. It clouds my judgment.

While lacking success in predicting my own or my family's future, I have had success predicting some of the worst tragedies of this new century. I predicted the airplanes going into the World Trade Center, for one. I always had an uneasy feeling about the towers, that they were in danger. I never felt safe inside them. I would find myself looking back at them after leaving and getting a strange feeling. I sensed they just weren't built correctly.

I get the same sensation about the plans to erect new buildings on that site. That land is now sacred ground. All the people who died there, their energy is still there. In my opinion, they shouldn't build anything to replace the towers. It should serve as a memorial only, so those who died will never be forgotten.

Another prediction was the December 2004 tsunami in Asia that killed thousands. I predicted that tragedy a year before it happened. I had forgotten I made the prediction until some of my students reminded me.

To tell you the truth, I've always had a bad feeling about the region. Why didn't officials have any type of early-warning system? It's happened many times before and yet they've never done anything about it.

Originally, I had predicted something big for Sri Lanka, and I foresaw several islands under water. I had told my students it would happen within a year and be the biggest natural disaster in our lifetimes.

An interesting aspect of the tsunami was that no animal carcasses were found among the human casualties except for such domesticated animals as dogs and horses, which had been tied up or caged when the tsunami struck. Other animals instinctively had sought higher ground before the wave hit.

I feel the reason the animals survived is because animals don't question their instincts. They sensed the vibrations. They just knew something was going on.

Human beings, on the other hand, rarely rely on their instincts these days. We let other people think for us. Need to know what's going on in the world, or even your own backyard? Check one of the many twenty-four-hour news channels, or log on the Internet. What to wear tomorrow? Tune in to the twenty-four-hour weather channel. We have all this information at our fingertips and we don't trust our own natural instincts. We don't know how to anymore. When was the last time you went with your gut feeling?

We are all born with instincts, but from the minute we leave the womb society seems to want to shake those instincts out of us. What is the first sensation once out of the womb? Someone smacking our backside, to get us breathing.

We come into the world stunned and scared. We go from a warm and safe place to the cold and unknown. We take our first breaths in pain. And the pain is from a stranger—a doctor—not someone who loves us.

Does a baby really need a slap to get it to breathe? God put us on this earth with all the tools to make it on our own. Sure, we need a good slap every now and then to keep us on the right path—that's where our parents come in—but we don't need someone to slap us every time we have to take a breath. We were born with the instincts to do that on our own, and when we do need help instinctively we go to the people who brought us into this world—our parents.

Even in the womb, we get to know our family by the sound of their voices. Before they see us and hear us, we hear them. We even hear the dog barking. While they're wondering if it's a boy or a girl, we're wondering what all that noise is out there.

That's why it's good for mothers to sing to their baby in the womb. Once out, the baby recognizes the mother's voice and immediately connects with her. The umbilical cord keeps the baby connected to the mother inside the womb, the voice keeps them connected outside. A baby hears that familiar voice and instinctively turns to his mother. Babies use their instincts from the moment they're born. It's a shame those instincts aren't nurtured.

When we are infants, our instincts are vital to our survival. But they are valuable for self-preservation throughout our lives. How successful we are at taking care of ourselves depends on how well we trust our instincts. Remember the animals that survived the tsunami.

Why did so many animals survive the disaster? Because they trusted their instincts and fled. The people no longer trusted their own instincts and look what happened. The animals felt the earth change and got out. The people didn't want to leave their material things behind, even if it meant risking their lives. Like so many people in Florida or Louisiana who refused to evacuate, to leave their homes. What could be so important in those houses to make it worth staying? Material things can be replaced, human lives can't.

Not everybody ignored their instincts when the tsunami hit. There were reports of villages that knew a tsunami was coming and evacuated in time. They were in tune with their environment, and they trusted their instincts. We all need to be *that* in tune with ourselves and the world around us.

Anyone can do it. And you don't even have to be psychic.

Some people are very intellectual. It is the "dance" they do in life. I believe that everybody has their own special dance. If we all had the same one, how interesting would that be? Imagine a Broadway show in which every actor danced the same dance, or sang the same song, for the entire show. How boring. How long would that show last? Life is the same way.

We all have our unique gifts, and that's what makes us so different from one another. We all have the ability to tune in to our instincts in our own way. It's just that some of us have learned to do it a little better than others.

My point here is, the sooner we learn to trust our instincts, the better off we'll be. While we may never have to face a life-or-death natural disaster—God willing—like the poor people in Asia did, we still have to be in tune with what our body and the world around us is telling us. Make sure your mind is open to your instincts, not closed.

One of the most fulfilling things about what I do is teaching others to trust themselves. People asked me for years to teach a psychic awareness class, so that I could reach more people, and finally I decided to do it.

In class, we sit around a table and we talk. We talk about whatever we like; in fact, you are encouraged to talk about whatever
is on your mind. You can say whatever you want; there is no
judgment.

I treat everybody the same no matter what comes out of their
mouths. What people say is often a good indicator of what is
going on with them and their universe.

I stress that the mind needs to be open, not closed. If somebody is a skeptic, it's hard to even sit down with him or her without arguing the whole time. As I said before, I'm not afraid of
skeptics or questions in regards to what I do—in fact, I welcome
them. But there's a time and place for that. I am willing to answer
any questions people have, especially my students. But I can't
teach them to the best of my abilities if there's someone present
who has an aura of negativity.

I tell students to use their own brains. While I may know more
about the psychic world than they do, I don't know it all. I never
think of myself that way. I am always learning, just like everybody
else. When students use their own brains, they find that, over
time, they are able to answer their own questions. They become
comfortable enough with their own abilities that they don't have
to rely on me.

I am not your typical schoolteacher, however. I have never
been shy or genteel. I don't mince words. I say exactly what is on
my mind.

When I first greet the class, I might use some sort of profanity to
break the ice, to get a good laugh out of everyone. (I do admit that I
have a very vile mouth. But you know what? I would rather hear

some curse word than, say, "cancer.") Once class begins, however, I'm all business. Psychic powers are nothing to play around with.

As I help students get in touch with their own abilities, I also teach them how to do out-of-body travel. I show them how to breathe correctly, how to use their senses. I show them how to pick up energy with their hands and feet. I also show them how to become aware of the inside of their body, so they can do some self-healing. I want students to walk away from my class feeling empowered, like they now know everything I know about being a psychic medium.

I don't want my students, in other words, to be like those clients who, after every reading, say without fail, "Yolana, I have just one more question." I want them to trust themselves, to look inside themselves to answer that next question. They have to learn to take care of themselves. They have to become important in their own lives. They have to take themselves seriously.

You have to know in your heart that you can do whatever you set your mind on. But you also have to really want to do it. If you are convinced it is what you want, no doubt you will accomplish it. But you first must believe you can do it. Then you pay your dues. The dues may be heavy, but, trust me, it's worth it in the end. Keep in mind that there are no free lunches in life and you'll be okay. And also keep in mind that this won't happen overnight, that it will take some time.

Time is a very difficult thing for a psychic to see. In the grand scheme of things, there is no time. If you want to plot your life on a time scale, you need to consult an astrologer, not a psychic medium. Astrology is the clock of the universe.

Time is a concept created by man. Time is all in your mind. You don't punch a clock when you enter or leave this earth.

Yet most of us get caught up in time. We always have to be here or there; we're always late for this or that meeting. We need to learn how to slow down and enjoy our time on this earth because, no matter who you are, we have only so much of it.

You should be worrying instead about finding out who you are, and why God put you here, instead of how much money you have, or how you're going to get your ex back in your life. You need to focus on the important questions.

But people don't realize this. Without fail, after every reading my clients always ask me, "Can I ask just one more question?" No matter what I've told them in their readings, there is always that one last question. And even after I answer that one more question, without fail, there is always just one more after that.

But when you look at life, isn't that what it's about? At the end, aren't we all going to have just one more question?

ELEVEN

Dying to Win the Lottery

I f you are so psychic," people ask me, "why don't you use your powers to win the lottery?"

It doesn't work that way. We would all hit the jackpot, if I was able to pick the winning numbers. I wouldn't keep it to myself; I love helping others. Unfortunately, there are different things that we are all supposed to go through and experience in our lives, so I'm sorry to tell you that not everyone is going to win the lottery.

With our "dollar and a dream" mentality, we think winning the lottery will be the answer to all our problems, that we will finally be happy. But it doesn't work that way. Trust me, money isn't the answer.

In fact, sometimes I feel more sorry for the rich than the poor because the rich often are so afraid of losing what they have.

They're afraid that without their wealth, people wouldn't like them. They are also afraid that if they don't have these material goods they won't be the same people. They worry that without their designer clothes or Gucci bags they will become nothing in the eyes of their friends and the public. They have grown accustomed to being catered to and the attendant flattery wealth brings. They become so obsessed with money and image that they lose sight of reality.

We all want to be praised, held, and loved, but none of that comes from money. Sadly, people with money don't know if they are being loved for their money or themselves. They may make a show of their money, in fact, hoping it's some kind of guarantee that people will at least like them for being rich. They don't realize that people love one another for what's on the inside, not the outside. To be fair, some poor people don't get this either.

One of my clients came to me after her mother died, upset that her mother had worked all her life, practically up to the day she died, and had nothing to show for it. She had spent every hard-earned penny on her family, never buying anything for herself. Her mother had died a poor woman, she felt.

But I personally knew the mother, and I told her daughter she was wrong. Her mother was far richer than most celebrities I knew. This woman left behind something that was so much more valuable to her family than money or material goods could ever be. She left behind a legacy of love. Money can run out after a while, but love is forever. It never dies. This woman fulfilled her destiny, in fact, in her love for her family.

Most people don't live life that simply. They want more, and they want it now. They want Ed McMahon to ring their bell to tell them they've become instant millionaires. Or they invest their hard-earned dollars in lottery tickets, hoping that ship will come in. And it better be the *Queen Mary*!

Over the years, I have read for people who, in fact, have been destined to win the lottery, and I told them. But if it wasn't the big jackpot, they acted like they didn't win at all, and even got mad at me, like I had something to do with the amount they won. I'm talking about $100,000 or $150,000, and they're upset it isn't a million. They're not satisfied with the gift given them. People focus too much on material possessions. We're spoiled. We have to have this and we have to have that, instead of concentrating on what's really important: our friends, our family, and our health.

Clients come to me with all kinds of problems. People come to me to pray for a sick or dying relative. Parents come to me to help them find their missing child. My heart just bleeds when I hear their stories.

And then there's the clients who want me to tell them how or when they will win the lottery. These are the readings that just drain me. Imagine me coming out of a reading where a family is in dire straits and going into another reading where the client is looking for the proverbial pot of gold at the end of the rainbow. The inequity becomes overwhelming at times.

We all have the pipe dream of being independently wealthy, of striding into that casino and pulling the handle on that slot machine that is going to come up with three cherries and our life changing forever. For most of us it remains a dream. We have to stop worrying about hitting the jackpot and concentrate on those things we can control. We need to control our destiny.

Some psychics want you to believe that they walk on water. I am here to tell you they can't. We're only human. People think that being able to read the past, present, and future must mean that we are brilliant, and that we lead perfect lives. I have lived far from a perfect life. I made my share of mistakes. Just because God gave me the gift of being able to read people's futures doesn't make me any better than you. As I have said before, my gift doesn't let me help myself. I live my life, like everyone else, by trial and error.

If a psychic tells you that you need her to break a curse or solve your problems, run—don't walk—the other way. You don't need a psychic for answers; the answers are all inside of you. As for paying hundreds of dollars to break a curse, what a scam! It's just another scheme to make a quick buck.

Beware of false prophets, in other words, because they'll just take advantage of you.

And not all false prophets come dressed in the robes of the psychic. Celebrities, pro athletes, people you idolize, may not be what they seem. Most wear a mask in public, and it's people's imaginations that elevate them to an almost holy status. We start looking to them for guidance in matters of politics, spirituality, even morality. Yet these people are no more capable of such guidance than you or I. Their fame and money doesn't make them wise.

Step back and look at who you're looking up to. Here are people who make themselves up so they look good to their public. They have little or no sense of reality. They have anything and everything their hearts desire. Yet with the exception of only a few, they don't make a real difference in the world. They do little to help those in need. They are very involved with themselves. They don't worry about anybody but themselves.

I had a very famous client who was concerned all the time that everybody wanted something from him. Why did everybody come to him for help? he asked me.

I told him he should consider himself blessed, that if I were in his shoes I'd be happy to be able to give so much.

But he didn't want to hear it. He didn't care about helping people. They were a bother, an intrusion in his life.

I am amazed how many people think life owes them. Life doesn't owe any of us anything. We owe life. We need to first give in order to receive.

I'm not saying we shouldn't look up to certain people. We can all benefit from role models, from mentors. Just be careful who you choose for a role model.

If you have questions about life, first question yourself. Try to find out what you are here for, what you need to learn. Don't look to someone else for answers just because of their status. Worship yourself and who you are. If you have questions, try to find the answers within yourself.

If you need guidance, seek out people who can really give it to you. Talk to a parent or minister or rabbi or teacher. The famous don't know or care about you; these other people do.

No one person is better than any other. Sure, we all need some guidance and help now and then, but be careful who you turn to. Everybody wants to look up to somebody, but I want you to learn to look up to yourself. Find your inner self and you've found your direction. Learn to trust your instincts and you'll be better off.

People want to know, if I'm so psychic why am I not rich. Why don't I play the stock market, bet on horses, or gamble in Vegas?

First of all, as a psychic, there are certain things I'm allowed to see and things I am not. Second, if we all got what we wanted when we wanted it, we'd have nothing to learn in life, and I'm a firm believer that we are put on this earth to learn. Third, I personally have no interest in playing the stock market or picking numbers every week for the lottery. I don't have the patience for that. I admit I played the lottery once, and lost, and, oddly enough, the numbers I played came up the next week. It's just not my karma to win. It's just not in the cards.

Speaking of cards, I do love to gamble. Josephine and I used to go down to Atlantic City to try our luck, but usually I would get frustrated and leave early. Also, it's just not that much fun for me.

For instance, I remember winning three hundred dollars one time in five minutes. Josephine was so excited, but then confused when I immediately left the table and cashed in my chips. She wanted to know why I was leaving in the middle of a hot streak. I explained to her that I could see other people's hands and it wasn't fair to the other players or the house. It was also bad for me karmically. Winning money dishonestly would one day come back to haunt me.

There also have been times when I've been asked to stop playing at a casino because I am a psychic. It happened one time when Josephine and I were playing the quarter slots and a host asked me to stop. They didn't allow psychics in the casino, he told me, and I had to go.

I had maybe thirty or forty dollars in my bucket at the time, not big winnings. I told him I had no control over the machines, that I had no idea which machine was going to hit. If I could pick which machines were going to hit, I added, I certainly wouldn't be playing the quarter slots! He didn't believe me.

Although I may not be able to pick winners for myself, I can for others. I speak with clients almost daily about stocks especially, them calling to ask "what I'm getting" on a specific stock or start-up company. Sometimes, I have no idea what I'm saying, telling them Company X is going to merge with Company Z for such-and-such reason, and they decide, based on that, which stocks to buy and sell. I find this amazing. Here I am, with only a grammar school education, advising high-powered business executives about stocks.

Clients want to know anything I'm "seeing" about a specific stock. I virtually can see the stock go up and down when I'm speaking with them. I tell them what I "feel" about the stock.

But stocks are difficult to predict. I may tell a client about a stock on the rise, but my timing may be off. I may be seeing something that's going to happen a month, a year, even two years down the road. Timing is everything when it comes to the market, and time is very difficult for a psychic to see. So even if I know a stock will rise or fall, I can't tell you when. What good is that?

Another subject I'm always being asked about is bad news, especially death. People's biggest fear when going to a psychic is that they'll receive bad news. I try to ease their mind by telling them that certain events are preventable, others are not. If I believe I can prevent something, I'll tell my client about it.

For example, if your aunt May is going to die soon, I won't say anything because I can't help. If, on the other hand, I see she is ill but I can help her get better, like if changing her medication will help her get better, I will say something. Then it's up to the client to see that May's medication is changed.

When people come to me and I see impending death, I'll advise them to consult their doctor if I think they are not ready to hear it from me. If I feel they are ready, I'll talk to them about death.

The time left is precious, I tell them, but there's also nothing to be frightened of. The one who dies doesn't suffer; it's the ones who are left behind that do.

When you die, there is no more pain. You no longer have a body to contend with. You've left your body—what I call your "space suit"—behind. You've left your suffering behind.

Over the years, I have taught several clients how to face death, but it is trying. No matter how many times I have done it, I am always drained emotionally and physically.

Years ago, a rabbi came to me after being diagnosed with advanced throat cancer. He didn't come to find out if the doctors were wrong or if I knew of any magic cure. He came because he was afraid of death. He had no idea what to expect, what was on the Other Side—if, indeed, there even *was* another side!

I placed a mirror in his hands and told him to look in it every day and tell himself that he could get well, that there was hope every day that he was still alive. This little suggestion helped him better cope until his illness became so advanced that he had to be hospitalized.

In the hospital, his fear of death became more pronounced, and we spoke many times about it. I am glad to say that, before he died, he finally faced his fears and was able to accept it and be at peace with himself.

I don't actually think the rabbi was so much afraid of dying as he was uncertain about what he should expect or do, as if there were a proper way to go about dying. No one knows how to die. None of us really has been taught anything about it. Sure, we know all about heaven and hell, that we'll go to heaven if we're good and we'll go to hell if we're bad. But none of us can actually picture ourselves dead.

People also ask me why, if God is so good, does He allow suffering? Why does He let an innocent boy be killed at twenty?

I answer that, karmically, it was the boy's time. He didn't know how to die gracefully. His karma was to have a short life so he could learn.

You learn to die by accepting it, by understanding the cycles of life and your part in it. His cycle had run its course.

We all have fears—whether it's death, abandonment, not being loved—and we all must face them. I have fears, but I think I'm learning that I shouldn't. I have experienced pain and I survived. I have found out the hard way that my purpose in life is to help others. This discovery has brought me peace. When I see my future, I see myself at peace. That is the greatest gift of all.

Some people think that because I'm psychic, of course I'm *always* at peace. But I'm human like everybody else, and I don't have all the answers—*especially* when it comes to me. It's lonely being psychic, because people rarely ask about my own well-being. They can't imagine how tough it is to tell someone he's going to die, or that a child is never coming home again.

It reminds me of a Barbra Streisand song called "Songbird," about a singer who always has a song for her audience in their tough times but who has no one to sing to her. Well, no one sings for me. This is one thing I've had to come to grips with and accept over the years. Ghosts, spirits, demons—even death—I can deal with. The loneliness is the worst thing.

Death is a gift, just like life is. When we cross over, we get a chance to look back and ask, "What have I achieved? What have I given? Have I overcome my fears?"

If we can answer these questions honestly, we go calmly. I experienced this transition when I was only ten years old with a near-drowning experience. When I lost consciousness, all the bad I'd done in my life flashed before my eyes.

Looking back, I believe I went through that horrible experience just so I could talk about it to clients later after I found my calling.

One day we all will experience death, but there is nothing to fear. Death is like birth. With birth, we leave the womb and are brought into the unknown. With death, we also go into the unknown, entering a new dimension. But be comforted by the fact that you do not face death alone. Others who have gone before you will be there to greet you. A loved one will help you make the transition.

But most people are scared to death of death. They go through three stages when facing it. First is denial: it can't happen to me. When they realize it can, they go to the second stage: bargaining with God. They try to cut a deal for more time. "If you give me more time, I'll . . ." When people realize that won't make any difference, they move to the final stage: acceptance.

Believe it or not, acceptance is the most peaceful stage of all. Accepting death allows you to actually *live* your last days instead of merely existing. You can enjoy the company of family and friends instead of worrying about what's on the Other Side and being alone. You realize that this isn't really the end, that some-day you'll all be back together again.

And that's comfort enough. That's hitting the *real* jackpot.

TWELVE

Mysteries
of the
Universe

While my intuition and ability connects me to the spirit world, I don't have the answers to all life's mysteries. I'm just as much a student as anyone else. And I still have a lot more to learn.

Not that I don't have opinions about a lot of things. But I'm not here to preach. I'm not here to tell you what to do, what to believe. I can only take you to the point where you can make your own decisions. We all have free will, after all, and we all are responsible for making our own decisions. How we live our lives is our choice.

I share thoughts with clients not to convince them to follow my lead but to get them to think, to engage their minds and get them to ask questions. But the only place they'll find the answers is within themselves. Only they can determine what is right for them, but first they must ask the question.

People frequently ask me about God. I believe in God. I believe He sets the stage for us, directs our destinies. But I also believe in free will. We may have a destiny, but we decide how to get there. The path we take is of our own free will.

Some religions would have you believe otherwise. They teach that we must follow their teachings to the letter or we will be punished—the biggest punishment of all being not going to heaven.

As a child, I was exposed to all sorts of belief systems, from Judaism and Catholicism to witchcraft and voodoo. While there is something to be learned from every religion, there are some things I just can't agree with. For instance, I believe in some teachings of Christianity, but I also believe in such Buddhist concepts as karma and reincarnation. There are some parts of the Bible I believe in and other parts I think are myths.

I believe in Jesus Christ. I believe He was a tortured soul who came to help the world. He was a teacher, a simple man, not royalty dressed in the finest robes. He was a human being who hurt and bled just like any other person.

Throughout His short life, He shared many messages with His followers, but I think the most important one was delivered at the Last Supper, and with His death. Before His death, He gathered together all His apostles and told them there was life after death. His resurrection would be the proof.

I believe Christ was really talking about reincarnation. He was saying that nobody actually dies; everybody comes back.

The Bible has been rewritten a number of times. One theory has it that the concept of reincarnation was originally part of Christ's teachings and was excised by someone later.

I think it makes perfect sense that reincarnation was originally part of the Bible. Christ talked about life after death, and rose from the dead to show it was possible.

I think the concept of heaven and hell was inserted in place of reincarnation. In my mind, heaven and hell are here on earth, not in the afterlife. In this life, what you put in is what you get back. Give and you shall receive. Do unto others as you would have them do unto you. You make your life here heaven, or you make it hell.

It's the same as karma. What you do in this life affects the next life. It's your choice. Only you can determine if you're in heaven or hell.

Christ came into this world to deliver a message. He simply wanted to share what He believed. Unfortunately, sharing what He believed led to His death.

I feel bad about what Christ had to suffer here on earth. And I feel just as bad for His mother, Mary, watching Him being tortured and finally crucified. No parent—not even the Mother of God—should see that. But Christ knew His purpose, and nothing could stop Him from fulfilling His destiny.

We too have a destiny. Sometimes we may wonder why we have to suffer to get there. I went through hell before finding my calling as a psychic. But even what seemed like insurmountable obstacles were just stepping-stones along the way.

If you don't believe in Christ, please don't discount what I'm saying. Whatever your belief system, the lessons are the same.

I'm not a big fan of organized religion. Religion is *not* God. Religion is man-made.

Throughout history, religion has been used to manipulate others. All religions are controlling in one way or another. They don't allow people to have their own beliefs. They want you to follow the teachings of the church, and that's it.

But I don't believe God wanted us to be sheep. He gave us a brain and free will. He wants us to use them to make our own decisions.

God doesn't care what religion you are. He doesn't care how often you go to church. He just wants you to be the best you can be as you travel on this journey known as life.

And what is man's place in the world? I'm often asked.

Man is just another animal. We may be more intelligent than animals, although when I read the newspaper or watch the news I often wonder just how much more. Look at all the ungodly acts that people commit everyday. Not even the lowest form of life on earth would ever do some of those things. Animals don't kill unless for food, or unless they feel threatened. Animals aren't selfish; they only tend to their immediate needs. Not like us humans who are constantly looking to acquire things, as if life were a competition—not caring about other people or the world around us. Who cares if we're destroying the environment with our pollution? What does it matter that we're using up all our natural resources, as long as we can drive our SUV's and build more high-rise apartments? Who do we think we are? What gives us the right?

When you look at a photograph of the earth taken from outer space, you see just how insignificant human beings are in the greater scheme of things. We can't even be seen from that altitude. The human race is just a minor part of the universe.

Speaking of the universe, there are so many things out there we don't really know about, but that doesn't stop us from thinking we do. Most of us, in fact, are clueless. We just take in as true all the information fed us by the media, Internet, etc., thinking everything is either black or white. The sooner we recognize that there are many shades of gray between, the better off we'll be.

People have to use common sense. They need to use their brains and make their own decisions. They need to discover what is right for them and what is wrong for them on their own. They can't live their lives according to what some religion dictates. They can't formulate a belief system according to the latest fashion. People need to live their lives the way they believe they should. Too many people make their life decisions based on what's in it for them, but they need to realize that it's not what you get out of life but rather what you put in that matters. There are bigger things in life than our own selves and our own needs.

People here on earth don't all think alike, that is for certain. What attracts one person may not attract another. We are all different. But in the grand scheme of things, we all are cut from the same cloth.

We all come into this world the same way. Given the choice, we probably would stay in the womb if we could. Why would you want to leave? We're safe, we're warm, we have everything we need. But we have no choice and must eventually leave the womb. We suffer through the pain of the birth process and enter a cold, strange, frightening world.

Our first exposure to life is pain. Although most of us are born to parents who will take care of us, we are equipped with a survival instinct. And we learn new things every day. We bang into things until we learn to avoid them.

We first crawl, then we learn to walk. But it takes courage to take that first step. And while we don't all learn to walk at the same time, we all learn to walk eventually. Sure, our parents may hold our hands at first, but soon enough we do it on our own.

The older we get, the more independent we get. By two years of age, we have a mind of our own, and we want to do things our way. We think we can make up our own mind, and we do whatever we can to get our way.

But our coolheaded parent nips our plans in the bud.

Older still, we cut the apron strings, making more of our own decisions, making more of our own mistakes. We sometimes decide something on our own just to show we're independent. Sometimes, we're just plain defiant, wanting to upset our parents.

Yet we are still scared at times. Will I be accepted? we wonder. Will I be liked? Or, worse, Will I be loved?

Despite all these different emotions, despite all the missteps, we keep trying different paths until we find the right one. When we do, then we really take off. And while we may take a side path or two along the way, we will eventually get where we need to go. In fact, these side paths are necessary to point us in the right direction. These wrong turns help us recognize when we have finally found the right path.

Relationships are an example of this. We may have to go out

with a lot of wrong people to find out what we *don't* want. And then when we do find the right person for us, we'll know it.

The truth is, we either are going to meet our ideal mate or we're not. But if we end up with the wrong person, or alone, we can't blame the universe. Believe it or not, we choose our fate.

We chose to be with the person we're with, even when that person is not right for us. And even though we know it's not right, we don't break it off. We get that funny feeling in our gut and signs are all over the place that something's wrong, but we ignore all the signs. And when we finally realize that this person isn't for us, it's usually too late, and the emotional—and some-times physical—damage has been done. I've seen this happen time and again to people when they ignore the universe's wakeup call. And history will keep repeating itself if we don't step in and make the right decisions for ourselves.

We should never ignore signs the universe is giving us. If a re-lationship or some other situation doesn't feel right, move on, start over. We're granted only so much time on this earth, and, before you know it, your time is up.

With death, as with birth, we pass through a tunnel. But this time, there's nobody on the other end to shake us up, to get us going. But we may get shaken up when we have to review our life and judge ourselves. We'll see everything that's right and wrong in this life, then decide what to do next.

We will see a bright light—called the "Blue Island"—where people go to recuperate and evaluate their life choices. We then decide when we will return to earth for the next life if we wish to repeat this life over again, to learn more. If we opt to repeat, our mission is to correct what we did wrong the last time around.

With reincarnation, we tend to choose the same spirits as companions over and over. Did you ever meet someone for the first time and say to yourself, "I have met this person before." Or we ask, "Where do I know you from?" We know he or she is a piece of the puzzle of our life, we just can't place the face.

One day, however, it all makes sense. Everybody we meet fits in somehow. Each teaches us something, but not necessarily what we want. And that's an important lesson, too. Knowing what you *don't* want is sometimes a better education than knowing what you do. The knowing is what reincarnation is all about.

The Blue Island is where you make peace with yourself. You will see people who you were with on earth who you want to see, and no doubt you encounter those you don't want to see. The Blue Island is all about choices: you choose who you want to be with. You choose what you want to learn this time around. You choose whether to come back at all. It's your call. While you're on the Blue Island, you dig down deep and ask yourself many questions, and if you feel there's more for you to learn you may decide to come back. You may think: "I've got to learn what rejection is," "I've got to learn what humility is," or "I've got to learn what charity is." And once you decide on whatever element or emotion it is you feel you need to learn in your next lifetime, you leave the Blue Island and return here.

If your lesson is money, almost certainly you will have the rug pulled out from under you financially. If your lesson is love, you will almost certainly have your heart broken. But when you finally learn your lesson, and embrace and come to respect who you've become, nothing else will matter. You will find you didn't need money to be happy, you didn't need someone by your side to be fulfilled. When you get to this stage, you also realize that nothing, nobody, can tear you down anymore.

Then life takes on new meaning. The key to life is learning to grow with each new experience. And once you know that, life isn't such a mystery after all.

THIRTEEN

Unleashing Your Psychic Powers

We are all born with different abilities and talents. Most people have the physical ability to sing, but not everybody has the talent to be the next American Idol. We may be able to string together words and sentences, but not able to write a best seller.

Similarly, I believe everybody comes into this world with the tools to be in tune psychically, but some of us are more connected with these abilities than others. Everybody is psychic to some degree, some to a much greater degree than others. We all choose our given ability before we are born. Apparently, I chose to be psychic.

I am able to pick up people's vibrations from photographs. Simply rubbing their pictures with my fingertips tells me what they are all about. If the photograph is of somebody who has died, I know it because of the absence of vibrations.

This phenomenon is called "psychometry." Psychometry is the ability to get an impression about something by holding it in your hand. The idea is that matter attracts matter. I can pick up something and tell you who it belongs to and where it has been. It's this ability that I use in police investigations, especially cases involving missing children.

You too can develop your psychometric perception. First, however, you must learn not to overanalyze, which can cause you to lose touch with the object you're holding.

Pick up an object and say the first thing that comes to mind. Don't think about it being right or wrong. That first impression is the valid one. Simply visualize with your mind and put what you see and feel into words. It's *that* easy.

Practice your psychometric skills not with photographs but clothing, jewelry, keys—anything. Relay your impression as soon as you grab hold of the object. When it has been "imprinted" by somebody else's vibrations, that person is going to register in your mind in some way. That is the definition of imprinting. Everything we touch we leave an imprint on, and the psychometrician can pick up on it right away.

Developing your psychic abilities is all about trusting your instincts. Sometimes after a reading, I can't believe what I've said. When I'm doing the reading, I say things one after another, like a play-by-play announcer for the Yankees. I may find some of it strange, but I don't censor myself because it might make sense to the client even though it doesn't make sense to me. I just say it like I see it.

When I teach my psychic awareness classes, one of the first things I have students do is exchange keys with somebody they don't know and hold them against their foreheads. Keys are very personal, especially since they usually are carried near the body, and they hold energy.

I ask the students to imagine what door the key unlocks. Then I ask them to unlock and go through that door and describe what they see.

Students who are truly in tune with their psychic powers are able to describe the room they've entered, the furniture in it, and maybe even what's on the table. They are not analyzing anything; they are acting as the messenger only.

By the time the course is over, I want students to be able to go through that door any time they want and describe what they see. I want them to be so in tune with their abilities that they can unlock any door.

When I investigate a murder case, I always ask police to bring me evidence—jewelry, clothing, keys—that was next to the body. It puts me immediately in touch with the case. I then can see with my psychic eye. It's not like seeing something with my regular eyes. It's like a projection of an image inside my head, onto a screen somewhere between my eyes.

Your psychic eye enables you to tap into the part of your brain that isn't analytical. In order to unleash psychic powers, you must tap into the part of the brain involving instincts, then come to trust those instincts—not an easy thing to do.

Most people these days are like robots, following the same daily routine year-round. God forbid they would have to rely on their instincts. Seems like everybody has forgotten how to use them.

Because people are so regimented, they don't like to go against the grain. Their own instincts may strike them as going against what they are used to, and they may dismiss them. They also don't want to be perceived as different from other people, don't want people talking about them.

I say, let them talk. "If they are not talking about you," my mother once told me, "then give them something interesting to talk about. Otherwise, you'll be damn boring." Give people something to talk about. You have to take chances in life. Trust your instincts and you won't go wrong.

I welcome both believer and skeptic alike with open arms. Clearly, I believe in the spirit world, and I see spirits of the dead walking around among us, something not everybody is comfortable with. And I understand people's reluctance to believe.

Not everybody who is dead can be reached. If he or she is still part of the spirit world, I can connect. If someone has reincarnated into a new life on earth, I can't. It usually takes spirits a while to reach the point of reincarnation, so chances are contact can be made.

What people don't realize is, they don't need me to put them in contact with their deceased loved ones; they can do it on their own, especially in dreams.

Clients will tell me they saw someone in a dream and it felt so real. That's because it wasn't a dream, I tell them, and then they look at me like I have two heads.

We all have the ability to make contact with the spirit world, I continue, and for many people it's easiest when asleep. When you're asleep, you can't analyze things. The analytical part of your brain shuts down for the night, and you tap into the psychic part of your brain.

I listened to the radio as a kid. The shows were entertaining, captivating, and powerful. The radio made you use your imagination. When you heard a door squeak or glass break, you would be scared, because your imagination brought the story to life, made things real, in your own special way. Likewise, everybody listening to that show had their own reaction.

Television and the movies don't allow this use of imagination. The scene is there for you to see, and nothing is left up to you. Everybody sees the same thing; everybody has the same reaction.

When you dream, it's like listening to the radio. Everything is more vivid; everything is more real.

Probably most people are receiving signs from spirits during the day that they are ignoring because their analytical mind tells them it doesn't make sense. When people are dreaming, the analytical mind shuts down and we acknowledge the signs.

Just like a spirit can travel anywhere, so you can, too. You can go out of your body when you dream. In our dreams, we can actually meet with the spirits of our deceased loved ones and communicate with them. If you wake up with a falling sensation, you are, in fact, falling back into your body after your travels. Your spirit is rejoining your physical body.

People come to me distraught, wanting to communicate with a deceased loved one. If I can connect with the spirit, the client leaves with a sense of calm, knowing that the deceased is fine in the spirit world but is also still in contact. They are even more comforted to discover they can connect in dreams. We all have this capacity to connect. We just don't use it. I hope these thoughts and insights will encourage you to get in tune with your own psychic powers.

I have been through a lot in my life, learned a lot along the way, and still have a lot to learn. And I still question why the spirits picked me for this job. Honestly, I don't have a clue.

Even though I've come a long way in life, I don't see myself as completed, and there is still a lot I want to do. I want to help the homeless because I was homeless. I want to teach people the place of money in their lives. All my life, the issues I dealt with centered on money. Why is money such an issue?

I learned the hard way you can't go through life without it. You have to eat, you have to pay rent, you have to have health insurance. You just don't have to worry about money all the time. I admit that this is something I'm still working on.

I am a human being like everybody else. Many people look on me as being different because I'm psychic, but I'm not. I am still a work in progress. But I have also come a long way. I've been to hell and back and am still standing. Not many people can say that.

I still worry about things. I still have self-doubt. But I've learned to use my strengths and deal with my weaknesses.

All except money. If I have it, I give it away. I don't feel it's important. I don't know if I'll ever change, but I'll keep working on these money issues. It's what I'm here to learn.

Since I have seen life from both sides of the coin, so to speak, I do have some perspective on the issue. I don't understand people who have nothing who don't try to make something of their lives. I also don't understand people who have everything who do nothing with it.

I especially don't understand the wealthy. They hoard their wealth. Their billions could help millions. And what about those people who throw away money on lavish houses, lavish things, lavish lifestyles? I'm not saying people shouldn't enjoy their money, but come on. Materialism, ultimately, is worthless, because, no matter how hard you try, you can't take it with you. Call me if you figure out how you can.

Every religion advocates giving money to charity. But most people don't do it. It's human nature to take care of yourself first, but it's also human nature to help others. Greed seems so prevalent in the world today, compassion seems all but lost. We don't need to compete with our neighbors. There will always be people who have more than you do. Your goal in life shouldn't be to catch up with them. It's far more important that you learn to do the most good with what you have.

We all have a lot of life lessons to learn while we are here on earth, but all of us should have compassion for other people, we need to care about them. So here is my advice to all of you: if something good happens to you, do something good for someone else. And if you want something good to happen to you, do the same thing. Good karma does come back to you.

Let's face it, most of us aren't going to appear in history books. If you are an artist, a sculptor, a writer, or a movie producer your creations may remain long after you leave this planet, but we all leave behind a legacy by what we do or don't do while we walk the earth. We are held accountable for our actions, either in this lifetime or the next. People must be more accountable for their actions in this lifetime.

I also want to tell you that no matter how strong you think you are, Mother Nature is stronger. Earthquakes, hurricanes, tsunamis: no one can do a thing to stop them. Nobody could stop Hurricane Katrina from hitting New Orleans. The earth is a living thing, and there is nothing we can do to control it.

But we can learn control ourselves. We can stop polluting our environment. We can stop global warming. We can let Mother Nature heal herself.

A vision that has come to me lately has to do with icebergs up in Alaska. I have dreamed about them at least three times, and I know what's going to happen: they are going to start going adrift. Like crazy. And cause all kinds of problems.

I also sense changes in store for California, that part of it is going to drop off into the ocean. I fear for the people who live there. It makes me sick to think about it.

My point is, we are going to have some big changes here on earth in the near future.

In truth, there is no place on the planet that is one hundred percent safe when it comes to Mother Nature. She's a gal to be reckoned with, and no man or woman—or animal, for that matter—can withstand her wrath.

We also need to pay closer attention to what we put in our bodies—what we eat, what we drink. Fast food is a problem. And there are also too many preservatives in things. People need to be more aware of what they are consuming.

Why are we getting new diseases? Look at what we're putting in our bodies. Just watch Morgan Spurlock's award-winning documentary *Super Size Me*. In it, the filmmaker ate nothing but fast food for an entire month. In the end, this fast-food diet takes him on a physical and an emotional roller coaster. It made him sick. You'll think twice next time before you head for the drive-thru.

The sad thing for me about trying to educate clients about what's going on in their lives is that I can't always get through to them. They come seeking advice about their problems, yet it seems to go in one ear and out the other. Why come for advice just to ignore it?

Other clients want to know about the future. Should I become a doctor? "Yes," I'll advise after reading, "become a doctor." A few years later, this same person is back. "Why didn't I become a doctor? You said I could become a doctor." Come to find out, he never went to college, let alone medical school.

People need to learn how to fend for themselves. They need to go out and become who they want to be. I can't do it for them. I can only tell them the options they may have. I can tell them about the windows of opportunity. But I can't make up their minds for them as to which path they should take. And I can't take that path for them.

Clients ask me all the time why their lives are miserable. But instead of asking me that question, they should be asking themselves. Only they can know their own souls. But they have to listen first. Ask yourself why once in a while and see what answers you get back from your own soul. What I often ask is, "Why do you so often settle for less?"

I also get clients who ask me, "Why am I going through this illness?" I often have to tell them it's because they chose that challenge when they chose this lifetime.

Some people actually decide to be sick. They like the attention. Or they decide they have nothing else in their world to live for but the disease. I know it sounds crazy, but there are actually people who will themselves to be ill. Some people convince themselves that they are sick, and they aren't happy until the doctor finds something wrong. But when the doctor finds something really wrong, they blame everything and everyone but themselves.

The body and the mind are two amazing machines, but keep feeding them garbage and they're bound to break down. If you keep thinking something's wrong with yourself, eventually something will be.

Life is full of whys. Most answers lie within the individual. But people don't want to be responsible for their lives. They want someone else to be. The truth is, we each chose our own path. We can't blame anybody else.

People are always coming to me for answers to their questions. For a change, I would like to turn the tables and ask them that inevitable one last question and see the answers I get back. I truly believe we all have psychic insights about ourselves, that the answers we seek are within ourselves. So the next time you have just one more question, take time out of your busy schedule to see if you can find the answer within yourself. I bet you'll find it was there all along.